North West Waterway Walks

Volume 2: Rambles by Mersey Waterways

David Parry

Published by Sigma Leisure – an imprint of
Sigma Press, 1 South Oak Lane, Wilmslow, Cheshire SK9 6AR, England.

British Library Cataloguing in Publication Data
A CIP record for this book is available from the British Library.

ISBN: 1-85058-383-8

Typesetting and Design by: Sigma Press, Wilmslow, Cheshire.

Cover photograph: Bradley Swing Bridge, Earlestown

Printed by: Manchester Free Press

General Disclaimer

Whilst every effort has been made to ensure that the information given in this book is correct, neither the publisher nor the author accept any responsibility for any inaccuracy.

Preface

This book presents for the reader a collection of twenty walks. They are based upon the numerous rivers and canals which flow into the River Mersey. Using a section of waterway for each walk, the book provides a guide to the exploration and enjoyment of the nearby countryside and to the delights which abound there in plenty.

Although each walk is accompanied by its own sketch map, the walker need only make a brief reference to it. The description of each walk has been made sufficiently detailed to allow for the maximum pleasure from a day out in the open air. All the walks make use of public rights-of-way as well as canal tow paths to which public access has been granted. No strenuous hill climbs are involved, giving the book an appeal to country-goers of all ages.

The Mersey waterways played a major role in the transformation of the North-West from a rural agricultural area into a modern industrial region. This book would be incomplete without some mention of the way in which the waterways developed and progressed. Within these pages can be found the stories of the waterway routes linked to the Mersey.

Highlighted for the reader's attention are the Sankey Canal – the first of all the English canals; the River Weaver – a working navigation passing through the Cheshire countryside; the Leeds and Liverpool canal – fifty years in the making and the longest single canal in Britain; the famous Bridgewater Canal – a waterway which set in motion a whole host of canal projects throughout the length and breadth of Great Britain; the Wirral and Chester sections of the historic Shropshire Union canal network, and the River Mersey itself – not simply a launching pad for Liverpool's maritime activity, but once part of a busy waterway link between Liverpool and Manchester, now peaceful once more.

The family of Mersey waterways, as well as helping Liverpool towards a position of maritime supremacy, assisted in the birth and development of other Mersey towns, each with its own individual character and traditions. Towns like St. Helens, Widnes, Runcorn and Ellesmere Port sprang directly from the industrial prosperity encouraged by the passage of a navigable waterway through their localities.

Within these pages can be found material which it is hoped will appeal not only to committed waterway enthusiasts, but to country walkers – experienced and beginners alike – who may be seeking new areas to explore and in which to enjoy what is becoming an increasingly popular form of relaxation and recreation. It is hoped that the historical information will be of interest to the general reader.

The Mersey waterways, vital transport routes for goods and passengers before the coming of the railway and the improvement of roads relegated them to a position of lesser economic importance, have now become ribbons of amenity and recreation available to us all, an historic legacy which is likely to become an even more pleasurable part of the landscape as the new millenium approaches. It is as an invitation to sample the many pleasures of these waterways that this book has been written.

The rambles start and finish within or near the Merseyside Transport Area. Public transport information is provided in a separate section. The route of each walk is accompanied by a sketch map. Places of interest, printed in **bold type**, relate to footnotes printed after the route guides.

David Parry

Contents

The Mersey Waterways   1

The Sankey Canal   1
The Liverpool Coal Crisis   2
Planning the new Waterway   3
The Sankey Canal is Built   4
The Operation of the Sankey Canal   6
Canal Improvements   7
The 1800s   7
The Canal under Railway Control   8
The Later History of the Sankey Canal   9
The Canal Today   10

The River Weaver   10
The Weaver in Victorian Times   13
A New Role for the Weaver   14

The River Mersey   15
A New Water Route   17
The Mersey & Irwell Navigation (1760-1804)   17
The Mersey & Irwell and the Bridgewater (1804-1830)   18
The Decline of the Mersey & Irwell Company   20
The Old Navigation and the Manchester Ship Canal   20

The Leeds & Liverpool Canal   22
The Leeds & Liverpool Canal before 1790   25
Completion of the Canal   27
The Leeds & Liverpool Canal (1816-1870)   28
Progress of the Leeds & Liverpool Canal after 1870   30

The Bridgewater Canal   31
The Bridgewater Canal (1776-1803)   33

The Bridgewater Trust   35
Before the Ship Canal   36
The Canal under Ship Canal Control   36
The Twentieth Century   37

The Shropshire Union Canal   38
The Wirral Line   38
Amalgamation and Progress   41
The Pressure of Competition   41
The Shropshire Union under Railway Control   42
The Shropshire Union after 1890   42

The Walks   44

1. **Garston – Oglet – Dungeon Point – Hale**   46
    Along the shore of the Mersey Estuary: 8 miles

2. **Hoylake – Meols – North Wirral Coastal Park – Leastowe –
    Lighthouse – Moreton**   53
    Between the estuaries of the Mersey and the Dee: 4¹/₂ miles

3. **Warrington – Howley – Paddington – Woolston –
    Martinscroft**   59
    Along the Mersey and Irwell Navigation: 6 miles

4. **West Kirby – Caldy – Thurstaston – Heswall**   65
    The Wirral shore of the River Dee: 7 miles

5. **Acton Bridge – Crowton – Pickering's Cut – Dutton Locks –
    Acton Bridge**   73
    A circular walk in the Weaver Valley: 8 miles

6. **Old Roan – Leeds & Liverpool Canal – Aintree Race Course –
    Melling – Netherton – Maghull**   79
    The fringe of the city and a visit to Melling village: 6 miles

7. **Maghull – Leeds & Liverpool Canal – Cheshire Lines Path –
    Lydiate – Leeds & Liverpoolcanal – Maghull**   84
    Visiting the Leeds and Liverpool Canal and the River Alt: 8 miles

8. **Lydiate – Hall Lane – Altcar Lane – Downholland –
    Leeds & Liverpool Canal – Lydiate**   89
    The fields and lanes of Lydiate and Downholland: 7 miles

9. **Downholland – Leeds & Liverpool Canal – Haskayne – Halsall – Leeds & Liverpool Canal – Downholland**   93
A further exploration of the Leeds & Liverpoool canal: 7$\frac{1}{2}$ miles

10. **Burscough Junction – Ring o'Bells – Hoscar – Prescott Bridge – Glover's Bridge – Burscough Junction**   98
The Rufford branch and main line of the Leeds & Liverpool: 8 miles

11. **Parbold – Gillibrand – Appley Bridge – Leeds & Liverpool Canal – Parbold**   103
A canal and country ramble along the Douglas Valley: 7$\frac{1}{2}$ miles

12. **Rufford – Old Hall – Leeds & Liverpool Canal – Sollom – River Douglas – Rufford**   108
A circular walk along the Rufford Branch and the River Douglas: 6$\frac{1}{2}$ miles

13. **Wigan Pier – Leeds & Liverpool Canal – Rose Bridge – Top Lock – Haigh Lower Plantation – Whelley**   112
A ramble around Wigan: 6 miles

14. **Blackbrook – Garswood Park – Chadwick Green – Carr Mill Dam – Blackbrook**   120
The countryside north-east of St Helens: 8 miles

15. **Blackbrook – Havannah Flashes – Penkford Bridges – Earlestown**   124
A chance to see reclamation of an industrial landscape: 5$\frac{1}{2}$ miles

16. **Sankey – Bewsey – Dallam – Winwick – Earlestown**   129
The Sankey Valley Park: 7$\frac{1}{2}$ miles

17. **Sankey Bridges – Fidler's Ferry – Widnes West Bank**   134
The Widnes section of the Sankey Canal: 5$\frac{1}{2}$ miles

18. **Ellesmere Port – Shropshire Union Canal – Stanney – Stoak – Croughton – Chorlton – Backford**   141
A waterways museum and the outskirts of Chester: 8 miles

19. **Chester – Shropshire Union Canal – Christleton – Rowton – Waverton Mill – Christleton – Chester**   149
The Cheshire section of the Shropshire Union: 6 miles or 8 miles

20. **Runcorn – Bridgewater Canal – Norton Priory – Preston Brook**   155
The Bridgewater and Trent & Mersey Canals: 8$\frac{1}{2}$ miles

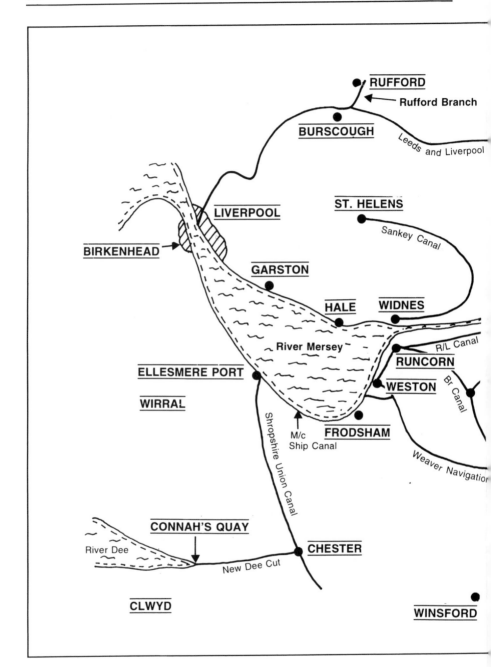

THE MERSEY WATERWAYS

To Leeds

L & L Canal

Canal

WIGAN

Manchester, Bolton & Bury Canal

LEIGH

Bridgewater Canal

SALFORD

WARRINGTON

Mersey & Irwell Navigation

MANCHESTER

Manchester Ship Canal

LATCHFORD

Bridgewater Canal

Bridgewater Canal

PRESTON BROOK

Trent & Mersey Canal

N

ANDERTON

Not to Scale

NORTHWICH

to Stoke

The Mersey Waterways

The Sankey Canal

The Sankey Brook is a narrow watercourse with its source to the east of St Helens. On its journey to the Mersey, the brook is joined from the north-west by three small tributary streams – The Windle Brook, Rainford Brook and the Black Brook. The Sankey Brook then flows eastwards, past Haydock and Earlestown, before winding its way to the south, passing under the Prescot – Warrington road at Sankey Bridges. After about a further half mile, the brook flows into the Mersey. Its southern section was sometimes known as Dallam Brook.

At a meeting of the Common Council of Liverpool held on June 5th 1754, the following order was issued:

". . . that two able and skilful surveyors be appointed to survey the Brooke commonly called Dalham brooke which empties itself near Sankey bridges in this county, such surveyors having first obtained the Licence of the principal Gentlemen or Land owners of the ground on each side of the said brooke, and that the expence thereof be paid by the Corporation".

The issue of this order led to the construction of the Sankey Brook Navigation, later known as the Sankey Canal or the St Helens Canal. The canal was the first English waterway to be built completely independently of tidal water, thereby laying claim to be the first true English canal.

The Liverpool Coal Crisis

The Sankey Canal was first built to relieve a chronic coal shortage at Liverpool which, by the year 1753, had assumed crisis proportions.

By 1750, Liverpool was beginning to take over from Wigan as the main industrial centre in South Lancashire. Although the growing prosperity of the town came chiefly from the ever-increasing tonnage of shipping passing through the port, Liverpool's industrial enterprises were flourishing too. Salt refineries operated on the Liverpool waterfront and at Dungeon Point on the Mersey shore near Hale. There was a glass works in the town, as well as sugar refining, brewing, and the manufacture of pottery. All these concerns needed a reliable supply of coal.

Liverpool in 1753 was exporting coal to Ireland and to other British ports. The export of salt, shipped down the River Weaver from Cheshire saltboilers, was of great importance to Liverpool's prosperity. The Liverpool merchants had to make sure that enough coal was being shipped up the Weaver to supply the Cheshire salt works. (In 1753 some 10,000 tons of coal was carried up the Weaver). Last, but by no means least, more coal was needed to keep Liverpool's rapidly increasing population warm in the winter months.

Until 1753 Liverpool's coal had been mined from pits in the Prescot and Whiston area. Efforts to find coal deposits closer to the town had proved fruitless. The Prescot district had supplied Liverpool for over a century. Coal was brought into the town via a ten mile journey by rickety horse drawn carts along the treacherous primitive surface of the Prescot – Liverpool turnpike road. In wet weather and in winter the road used to get into a deplorable condition; coal carts often could not get through to Liverpool at all.

Two events sparked off the Liverpool coal crisis of 1753. Firstly, the turnpike trustees of the Prescot road increased their tolls. Secondly, the owner of the Prescot Hall colliery raised his prices by one-fifth. At one fell swoop, Liverpool coal merchants had to pay more to bring the coal into the town, as well as paying a higher price at the pithead. The resulting shortage gave rise to rioting and public disorder in Liverpool. The Corporation had to think long and hard to resolve the crisis.

Their solution was to get coal from other pits and, secondly, to bring it to the town along a route as yet unexploited – a new artificial waterway leading from collieries in the Parr and Haydock districts near St Helens to the Mersey estuary. This new waterway was the Sankey Canal.

Planning the new Waterway

Liverpool Corporation instructed Henry Berry, the Liverpool Dock Engineer, to make a survey of the Sankey Brook with a view to making it navigable by widening, deepening, and by straightening its course using artificial short cuts and the construction of locks and weirs. Henry Berry, assisted by William Taylor, carried out a survey during the summer of 1754. Under the tutelage of Liverpool's first Dock Master, Thomas Steers, Berry had gained a wide knowledge of water engineering. He had relatives in Parr and had spent much of his childhood there. It is more than likely that he already was familiar with the Sankey Brook and the neighbouring countryside.

The two chief supporters and promoters of the Sankey Brook improvement were John Ashton, the owner of the Dungeon salt refinery, and John Blackburne Jnr., who owned the Liverpool salt works as well as several Cheshire salt pits. It is likely that these two men had formed a business alliance with Miss Sarah Clayton, who had inherited the Parr Hall estate. Miss Clayton had recently, in 1742, laid out Liverpool's Clayton Square on fields she owned there. She was a lady of great influence in Liverpool business circles. As owner of coal-bearing land in Parr, she had, like Ashton and Blackburne, a powerful interest in the new waterway.

In October 1754 Liverpool Corporation agreed to lend £300 to Ashton and the other promoters towards the cost of drawing up a Bill and getting it through Parliament. On November 14th, 120 five-pound shares were offered for sale at the Mayor's office in the Liverpool Exchange. The Bill had a smooth passage through both Houses of Parliament and became law as the Sankey Brook Navigation Act (28GeoIIc8) on March 20th 1755.

The Sankey Canal is Built

Although the 1755 Act authorised the promoters to make the Sankey Brook navigable, the paradox is that at no time was any work done on the brook itself. It remained unnavigable and unimproved. Instead, a canal was cut, alongside and almost parallel with the old brook. A clause in the enabling Act, intended to allow for improvement of an existing waterway, reads:

"the Undertakers .... are hereby authorised and impowered... to make such new Cuts, Canals, Trenches, or Passages for Water, in, upon, or though the Lands or Grounds adjoining or near unto the same River... as they shall think proper and requisite".

The promoters conveniently interpreted the clause to allow for the construction of a canal. Henry Berry began to build what was, in effect, a single new cut, the Sankey Canal, alongside the Sankey Brook.

The first canal section, opened to traffic in 1757, ran from the Mersey to Parr, a distance of some seven miles. Eight locks were built to raise the water level gradually. If the Mersey tide was favourable, a vessel could enter the canal through the **Sankey Lock**. To reach Parr, it then passed through seven other locks: **Bewsey Lock**, situated a few hundred yards to the east of Bewsey Old Hall; **Hulme Lock** at Dallam; **Winwick Lock**, about a mile west of that town; **Hey Lock**, south of Newton; **Bradley Lock**, north of Bradley Old Hall; **Newton Common Lock**, situated a short distance west of the present Sankey Railway Viaduct, and **Haydock Lock**, about a mile south of the village.

The Old Double Lock, completed in 1759, was the first of its type in Britain, so called because it had a pair of rises in level, forming a staircase. By 1759 the canal had completed to Gerard's Bridge. 1762 saw the opening of the **Blackbrook Branch**, which led off from the Old Double Lock towards the present site of Carr Mill Dam. Ten years later, in 1772, a branch running southwards from the Gerard's Bridge section was completed as far as **Boardman's Bridge**. Another staircase lock, known as the **New Double Lock**, was built at Pocket Nook. Water for the canal was supplied by tapping the Sankey Brook and its tributary streams. If the water level rose too high, excess water was allowed to flow through spill-over weirs into the brook. When opened, the canal was five feet deep and navigable to boats of 35 tons.

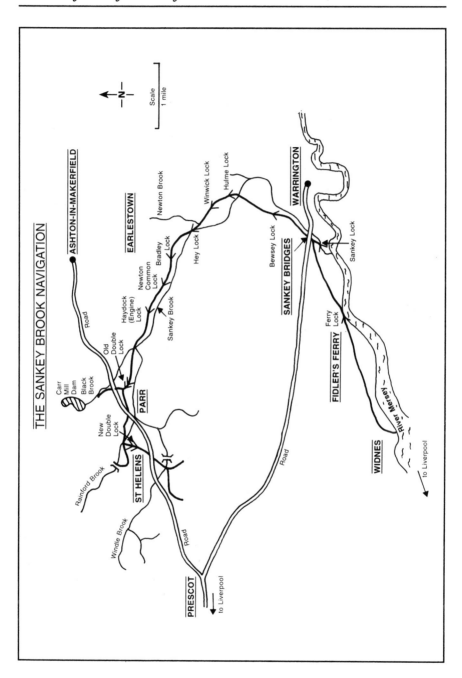

THE SANKEY BROOK NAVIGATION

ASHTON-IN-MAKERFIELD

EARLESTOWN

Newton Brook

Winwick Lock

Hulme Lock

WARRINGTON

Bradley Lock

Hey Lock

Bewsey Lock

SANKEY BRIDGES

Sankey Lock

Newton Common Lock

Haydock (Engine) Lock

Sankey Brook

Road

Old Double Lock

Ferry Lock

FIDLER'S FERRY

Carr Mill Dam

Black Brook

New Double Lock

PARR

ST HELENS

Rainford Brook

WIDNES

River Mersey

to Liverpool

Windle Brook

Road

Road

PRESCOT

to Liverpool

Scale
1 mile

N

The Old Double Lock on the Sankey Canal

The Operation of the Sankey Canal

Although Sarah Clayton had a virtual monopoly of the Sankey coal trade in the 1760s, she was not without rivals in the St Helens coalfield. In 1756 Robert and John Tarbuck opened mines at Windle on lands leased from the Gerard family. The Tarbuck brothers operated until their lease expired in 1768. In 1765 Sir Thomas Gerard, the owner of the Garswood Park estate, began to send coal down the canal. John Mackay, who opened a series of pits at Ravenhead in 1768, succeeded in attracting new industries, fed with his coal. The British Cast Plate Glass Company opened there in 1776, thereby launching the St Helens involvement in glass manufacture. In 1779 the Pary Mine Company came from Anglesey to Ravenhead and opened a copper smelting works, the forerunner of the Ravenhead Copper Works.

Sarah Clayton was declared bankrupt in 1778 and died the following year. Coal going down to Liverpool along the canal was supplemented by cargoes arriving via the new Bridgewater Canal at Runcorn. After the Leeds & Liverpool Canal was opened in 1774, coal was brought into Liverpool from the Wigan coalfield.

Canal Improvements

As early as 1762, boatmen began to experience great difficulty in getting their boats up into the canal at the Sankey entrance lock. The silting of the brook below the lock was worsening. No amount of dredging could ease the situation. Vessels could reach the lock during spring and average tides, but failed to enter the canal at the low 'neap' tides. An additional hazard was the constantly changing position of the navigation channel of the Mersey above the Runcorn Gap. Shifting sandbanks regularly caused craft to run aground. To solve these two navigational hindrances, the Sankey Navigation Company extended the canal from Sankey Bridges, through the Penketh Marshes to Fidler's Ferry, thereby avoiding the brook altogether and reducing the journey by about $1^1/_2$ miles.

The 1800s

By 1800, over thirty coal mines had been opened in the four St Helens townships of Eccleston, Parr, Sutton and Windle. In that year, some 80,000 tons of coal were being carried down the canal on flat-bottomed sailing boats. At a meeting at the Fleece Inn at St Helens in January 1830, the St Helens Railway Company was launched. The company built a rail link from a number of St Helens collieries to a dock on the Mersey shore at West bank, Widnes. The new railway dock was opened in July 1833; it could accommodate coal boats of 300 tons. Forty such boats could berth at the dock at any one time. The Sankey Canal Company faced the prospect of competition from the railway. In the summer of 1833, 2,000 tons of coal a day were being shipped out of the West Bank railway dock, most of it up the Weaver into Cheshire, the rest to Liverpool and to Ireland. Salt and ores for the glass, iron and copper factories were moved northwards from the dock terminal to St Helens.

In response to railway competition, the Sankey Canal proprietors built a further section of their waterway, from Fidler's Ferry, parallel to the

Mersey for about $2^1/_2$ miles to reach the river at a new dock of their own at Widnes. The company opened the extension and new wharves on July 24th 1833, just two days before the official opening of the railway company's new Widnes dock.

The Canal under Railway Control

After the opening of the two separate Widnes docks in 1833, the Sankey Canal and the St Helens Railway became embroiled in competition for the transportation of goods. Both companies reduced their prices in attempt to seize each other's traffic. Neither could really afford to engage in a price war, but no agreement could be reached between them. Both found it difficult to make ends meet.

In 1838 the canal company approached the railway with a view to a possible amalgamation. A proposed merger was rejected by the railway company's shareholders, who decided to soldier on. In January 1844 the companies agreed that it would be to their mutual advantage to join together. In July 1845 the railway paid £144,000 to amalgamate with the canal as "The St Helens Canal & Railway Company".

The new regime managed to keep its head above water for nearly twenty years. The tonnage carried on the Sankey Canal averaged about 450,000 tons annually, compared with 170,000 tons in 1836. Several new pits had opened around Blackbrook. These were not linked to the railway and so their coal went by canal, thereby boosting its tonnage.

The combined company opened a dock at Garston in 1852, connected by a new railway line to Widnes, where the old canal dock was kept open. The canal continued to operate with three points of access to the Mersey: at Widnes wharf, Fidler's Ferry and at Sankey Bridges, although by 1850 the latter entrance was rarely used. Its lock gates were allowed to fall into disrepair and were not renewed.

Under the provisions of an Act of 1861, the St Helens Company was taken over by the London & North-Western Railway Company. There-after, the Sankey Canal's administration was only a small part of a large railway concern. By 1870 the heyday of the canal had passed. It con-tinued to operate, carrying little or no coal and relying for traffic upon materials passing to and from St Helens and the blossoming industrial belt at Widnes: chemicals, salt and metal ores.

The Later History of the Sankey Canal

During the second half of the 1800s, the St Helens coal which used to be carried on the canal was transferred to the railway, with the result that by 1900, no coal at all was being carried on the waterway. There were raw materials for the St Helens factories: sand, alkalis, acids and salts for the glass industry, and sugar for the refinery at Earlestown. Large quantities of stone and gravel for roadmaking and repairs were offloaded at the various wharves and quays along the canal. There was also a sizeable tonnage of limestone and manure for use on the land.

After 1880, the canal tonnages began to fall with increasing speed. Some 500,000 tons were carried in 1888. Ten years later the figure was 380,000. By 1905 it was below 300,000 and the canal thereafter ran at a loss. Very few boats travelled all the way to St Helens after 1910. The last St Helens-bound cargo was carried in 1919.

The Railways Act of 1921 transferred ownership of the canal to the London Midland & Scottish Railway Company. It was clear that there was no longer a need for the canal in St Helens. Goods and materials were being handled by road and rail. In 1930 the St Helens Corporation, in co-operation with the parent railway company, held an inquiry into the canal. The corporation wanted to widen several roads in the town and needed to convert the narrow swing bridges into larger, fixed structures. The L.M.S. saw an opportunity to cut its losses on canal maintenance. Consequently, in 1931 the canal was closed to navigation above Newton Common Lock.

By 1930 the annual tonnage had fallen to 94,000. In 1946, the first post-war year, only 20,000 tons were carried. During the 1950s the canal entered its final phase as a commercial waterway. Lead ore was carried to a chemical works at Sankey Bridges and raw sugar continued to be delivered to the refinery at Earlestown. In 1959 the sugar consignments were sent by road and all commercial traffic ceased. The waterway was abandoned by the British Transport Commission in 1963.

The Canal Today

Following closure, most of the Sankey Canal has continued in use as a water supply and drainage channel. During the 1970s the section between Newton and Bewsey was dewatered and converted into farmland. Several sections in St Helens were filled in and built over. At present, most of the canal remains in water and forms part of the Sankey Valley Country Park. The old industrial wastelands along the canal have been progressively landscaped to blend with the two waterways – canal and brook – forming a ribbon of countryside extending from Carr Mill, past Newton, Sankey Bridges and Fidler's Ferry to the Mersey shore at Spike Island in Widnes.

The River Weaver

". . . The making of the River Weaver alias Weever alias Wever navigable for Boats, Lighters, and other Vessels, from Frodsham Bridge in the County of Chester to Winsford Bridge in the same County will ... be very beneficial and convenient, as well for the Carriage of Salt and Cheese (the great Manufactures and Produce of the said County) as of other Goods and Merchandizes to and from the Towns and Parts adjacent..."

The above passage is an extract from the preamble of the River Weaver Act of 1721. The Act signalled the beginning of the river's life as a working navigation. The Weaver retains this role today; it is one of the eleven B.W.B. waterways classified as 'commercial'.

Nowadays, local traffic has been replaced by international traffic to the two I.C.I. chemical works at Winnington and Wallerscote and, until recently, to the British Waterways Board's depot and wharf at Anderton. However, until the 1930s, the traditional traffic on the Weaver was coal and, more essentially, Cheshire salt. During the peak years between 1870 and 1890, over a million tons of rock salt, mined at Northwich and Winsford, were carried down the Weaver into the Mersey each year, most of it for export.

The impetus behind the conversion of the old river into a navigable waterway had its origins as far back as 1670 when, at Marbury near

Northwich, John Jackson was prospecting for coal on behalf of the lord of the manor, William Marbury. His drill unearthed a sample of hard crystalline rock salt. As a result of his discovery, Cheshire salt, which for centuries had been purified locally from natural brine springs, needed no longer to be purified in the county. It could be exported in the form of rock salt (the kind still used in road gritting) and refined elsewhere,

Improvement work on the river began in 1729. By 1732, sailing flats were passing to and fro between Frodsham, Northwich and Winsford. Coal went upstream; purified 'white salt' and unrefined rock salt passed downstream to the Mersey. By 1742 there were eleven locks and weirs on the navigation – at **Pickering's Boat, Dutton Bottoms, Acton Bridge, Saltersford, Winnington, Northwich, Hunt's, Hartford, Vale Royal, Newbridge** and **Butty Meadow**. (See map).

However, by 1757, the year in which the Sankey Canal was opened, maintenance of the Weaver had been so badly neglected that Liverpool Corporation put a takeover bid to the Weaver Commissioners, who, after a great deal of wrangling, rejected the offer. The following year, in 1758, Henry Berry, fresh from his successful construction of the Sankey Canal, was put in charge of a £5,000 improvement scheme for the Weaver. The scheme included new short cuts at Pickering's and Saltersford and a new lock above Frodsham. (The latter was aimed at preventing the troublesome stranding of boats at neap Mersey tides).

In March 1759, disaster struck. The bank of Berry's new cut at Pickering's collapsed. Three days later, a rock salt pit beside the navigation also caved-in, taking Northwich lock down with it. The following year, 1760, after Pickering's weir had been washed away too, Berry, now understandably well out of favour with his Cheshire masters, was dismissed and replaced as Chief Engineer by Robert Pownall. In 1760 also, management of the navigation was put on a firmer footing by the formation of a new governing body of 105 Trustees. Finances immediately improved. By 1777 the navigation more than broke even. The first profits were transferred into the Cheshire county treasury. New cuts at Barnton (1771) and at Acton Bridge (1778) were followed by the long-awaited new lock and cut at Frodsham (1779) and, in the 1790s, by new cuts at Vale Royal, Newbridge and Hunt's.

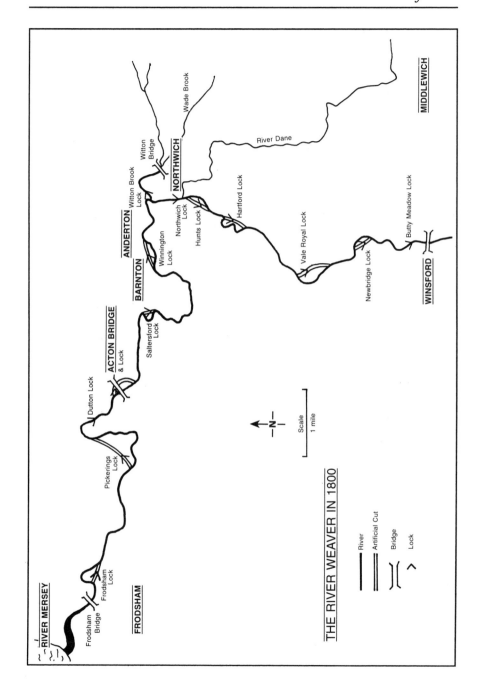

THE RIVER WEAVER IN 1800

Scale
1 mile

River
Artificial Cut
Bridge
Lock

In the 1760s the Weaver Trustees fought a losing battle to get the new Trent & Mersey Canal connected to their river. Instead, an Act of 1766 sanctioned a junction between the Trent & Mersey and the Duke of Bridgewater's Canal at Preston Brook. When it was opened in 1777, the new canal ran for some miles parallel and close to the Weaver. Nevertheless, despite a lean decade caused by competition from the Trent & Mersey, by 1789, because of increasing tonnages of salt and coal, the Weaver became profitable again.

The Anderton Canal Basin, completed in 1798, allowed for transhipment of goods from narrow boats on the Trent & Mersey to larger sailing flats on the Weaver. In 1810 the trustees cut a new short canal, called the Weston Canal, from the Weaver to the Mersey. The new waterway, by running across Sutton Marshes, allowed vessels to bypass the mouth of the Weaver and reach the deep water of the Mersey at Weston Point.

The Weaver in Victorian Times

In the 1840s, under the direction of the engineer William Cubitt, the river was deepened and the lock chambers, now converted from wood to stone, enlarged, allowing the passage of vessels of 150 tons. Some locks were doubled to allow two boats to pass each other while going through them, thereby saving valuable waiting time. By 1865, every lock on the navigation had been doubled.

In 1865 also, the Trustees asked their Chief Engineer, Edward Leader Williams, to draw up a scheme for making the Weaver capable of accommodating sea-going vessels. A new Delamere Dock at Weston was completed by 1870 and coastal vessels began to come up-river. In 1871, work began on the enlargement and deepening of the locks. Their number was reduced to four only – at Dutton, Saltersford, Hunt's and Vale Royal. Each lock is 220 feet long and 42ft 6in wide, with a water depth of 15 feet in its chamber. The new locks were paired off with the 100ft x 18ft locks built in earlier years. Passage of vessels through the locks was speeded by push-button operation of turbine-driven lock gates. Ships could then rise in level, via four lockings only, by $37^1/_2$ feet between Sutton Lock and Winsford Bridge, a distance of $16^1/_2$ miles.

The year 1875 saw the opening of the Anderton Lift, allowing the transfer of laden vessels to and fro between the Weaver and the Trent & Mersey. The lift consists of two large containers, known technically as 'caissons', which hold the floating boats. The containers move on hydraulic rams which fit into underground cylinders. As one container rises, the other falls, lifting or lowering a boat as required. The lift was designed to transfer one canal barge or two narrow boats in single operation. Although it underwent an overhaul in its centenary year of 1975, later inspection revealed that the old metal superstructure had become unsafe and the lift had to be closed down. For some years a campaign has been underway to get the lift restored to working order but, at the time of writing, none of the necessary expensive reconstruction work has been started.

A New Role for the Weaver

After 1885, despite an improvement of facilities at the Weston Point terminal by the opening of the Tollemache Dock that year, the salt trade on the Weaver declined. Traffic was gradually being lost to the railway network. By 1900 the Weaver was replacing its salt trade with an increasing tonnage of chemicals and raw materials for the Potteries. After 1910, when the Salt Union opened a pipeline to pump brine direct from the saltfields to its factory at Weston, salt traffic on the river nosedived.

During the inter-war years 1919-1939, the navigation, now based upon chemical traffic, remained profitable. The Weaver's continued success contrasted sharply with the dwindling commercial viability of the other Mersey waterways. The Weaver, being a river navigation rather than a tightly constricted canal, could easily be deepened to accommodate larger vessels. In the 1800s the Weaver Trustees had seen to it that their navigation was continually upgraded; they had, from their huge salt traffic, sufficient funds to pay for improvements. When the salt trade disappeared, the Weaver Navigation was already well equipped to meet more modern requirements.

The river began to carry coastal vessels of increasing capacity. Several bridges over the waterway were altered to allow for the passage of the higher masts and superstructure of the larger merchant ships. A swing bridge at Sutton Weaver, completed in 1923, was followed by one at Acton Bridge in 1932. In 1938 a new high level bridge was completed at Hartford, thereby preserving navigation through to Winsford.

In 1948 the Weaver was nationalized and taken under the control of the British Transport Commission. Weston Point docks were converted into a container terminal. After 1945, only chemicals were carried on the navigation. However, after 1950, processed salt was shipped down to I.C.I. Runcorn factory on the east bank of the Weston Canal. After the British Waterways Board took control in 1962, the navigation was deepened and Anderton depot modernized to take coasters.

Weaver cargo tonnages have remained steady since the 1960s. Although the river is a working navigation, pleasure cruising is popular. The river's banks provide, as they have for centuries, numerous opportunities for enjoyable walks through some peaceful and beautiful parts of the Cheshire countryside.

The River Mersey

The Mersey is formed by the mixing of the waters of three other rivers – the Goyt, Etherow and the Tame. The Goyt and the Etherow come together some four miles east of Stockport. When their combined flow mixes with the Tame at Stockport, the resulting waterway takes the name 'Mersey'. From Stockport, the narrow Mersey winds a westerly course through Greater Manchester, passing through Cheadle, Gatley, Northenden, Sale and Ashton-upon-Mersey. It then winds past Flixton and Carrington before flowing eastwards towards Irlam. About a mile south of Irlam, the river slides over a weir into the Manchester Ship Canal and thereby loses its identity completely. The Mersey reappears from the ship canal some six miles downstream, near Rixton Old Hall. The river then twists and turns past Woolston and Latchford. On reaching Howley, the Mersey flows over another weir into the tidal flow of its estuary. After passing under Warrington Bridge, it widens out towards Fidler's Ferry, before narrowing again to run beneath the road bridge at the Runcorn Gap. The estuary then gradually broadens before swinging to the north-west, narrowing again, and flowing between Liverpool and the Wirral into Liverpool Bay.

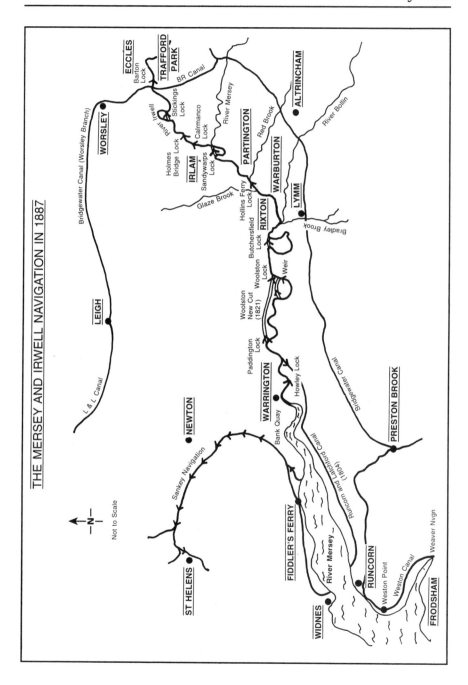

THE MERSEY AND IRWELL NAVIGATION IN 1887

A New Water Route

In 1721 an Act of Parliament authorized the newly-formed Mersey & Irwell Navigation Company to improve the two rivers and thereby create a navigable water connection between Liverpool and Manchester. The company was empowered to straighten and deepen the Mersey and the Irwell by making new cuts, building protective floodbanks and laying a towing path. The company could build new locks and weirs and could *"demolish any Mill, Wear, or other obstruction which may obstruct or hinder the Navigation"*. A maximum toll of 3s 6d ($17^1/_2$p) per ton of cargo was sanctioned for a journey of any distance along the navigation, which extended from Warrington Bank Quay to Hunt's Bank in Manchester.

The first improvement work on the Mersey and the Irwell began in 1724. By 1736, vessels could sail to and fro between Liverpool and Manchester and intermediate places along the new waterway. Based upon a survey and plan drawn up by Liverpool Dock Master, Thomas Steers, eight new locks, each positioned alongside a weir, were built to negotiate the rise in water level between Liverpool and Manchester, separating the navigation into seven distinct stretches of water. The eight original locks, encountered by a boat sailing in the Manchester-Warrington direction, with their rises, were: **Throstle Nest** (7ft 6in), **Mode Wheel** (5ft 10in), **Barton** (5ft 9in), **Stickings** (near Daveyhulme, 4ft 4in), **Holmes Bridge** (near Flixton, 5ft 2in), **Calamanco** (3ft 3in), **Partington** (Hollin Ferry, 6ft 6in) and **Howley**. (The last-named lock connected the navigation to the tidal waters of the Mersey; its rise varied with the state of the tide). (See map on page 16). All but one of the eight original lock sites were obscured by the construction of the Manchester Ship Canal, which swallowed up most of the navigation. However, Howley Lock can still be seen, some 200 yards upstream of Warrington Bridge. The weir at Howley still marks the tidal limit of the Mersey.

The Mersey & Irwell Navigation (1760-1804)

The opening of the Bridgewater Canal's connection to the Mersey estuary at Runcorn in 1776 confronted the 'Old Quay Company' of the Mersey & Irwell with a powerful rival for the Liverpool-Manchester carrying trade. Because the Bridgewater was a dead-water navigation, it had none of the drawbacks of a semi-natural watercourse like the

Mersey-Irwell. Floods, droughts and tidal difficulties did not hinder the Bridgewater. Moreover, the Manchester-Runcorn distance was about 30 miles on the Bridgewater – a good deal less than the length of the meandering Mersey-Irwell river system. Although the Navigation Company made no profit until the 1790s and were constantly short of funds for the maintenance and improvement of their rivers, two new locks and short cuts were built in the 1760s – at **Sandywarps** (near Irlam) and at **Butchersfield** (near Rixton).

By 1779 the financial position of the Mersey & Irwell Company was far from healthy. To avoid further difficulties, the proprietors sold out to a new consortium of men from Liverpool and Manchester. The purchasers paid £10,000 for the five hundred company shares. After 1790, owing to a rapid increase in traffic between Liverpool and Manchester, the Old Quay Company, like its neighbour the Bridgewater, entered a period of prosperity. Shareholders then included several prominent Liverpool figures – John Blackburne, owner of the Garston salt refinery; Thomas and John Tarleton and Daniel Backhouse, former partners in the slave trade; William Gregson; and the Heywood brothers – Arthur and Benjamin – the founders of Heywood's Bank in Liverpool's Water Street. Another shareholder in 1794 was Francis, Duke of Bridgewater, using his ownership of Mersey & Irwell shares to get useful first hand information on the activities and plans of his rivals.

By the 1790s the water level in the Mersey between Warrington and the Runcorn Gap had fallen so low that boats were regularly stranded there for days on end. To solve the problem, the Mersey & Irwell Company built a canal between Runcorn and Latchford. It came to be known as the 'Old Quay Canal' and, around Latchford, as the 'Black Bear Canal' (after the local inn). The Runcorn & Latchford Canal, $7^3/_4$ miles long, was opened in the summer of 1804, enabling cargoes to be moved from Liverpool to Manchester within two days.

The Mersey & Irwell and the Bridgewater (1804-1830)

By opening its new Runcorn & Latchford Canal in 1804, the Mersey & Irwell Company had shortened the Liverpool-Manchester journey along the old navigation to 28 miles – exactly the same as that via the

Bridgewater Canal. Transfer of carrying companies' allegiance from the Bridgewater to the old navigation resulted in a fall in Bridgewater profits. The Mersey & Irwell Company introduced passenger services. These were more convenient than those on the Bridgewater, whose passengers had to trudge their way up or down the flight of locks to the Mersey estuary at Runcorn. Transfer between boats at the Old Quay Basin at Runcorn was the more simple matter of walking a short distance along level ground.

The 1807 edition of **Gore's Liverpool Directory** printed this advertisement for services on the old navigation via the new Runcorn & Latchford Canal:

"In consequence of the late improvements made in this Navigation, the delays formerly occasioned by neap-tides are now wholly done away. Vessels sail daily for the Carriage of Goods and Merchandize between Liverpool and Manchester, with the greatest dispatch, safety and care".

"Packet Boats for Passengers and their Luggage are also now established to pass between Runcorn and Manchester, and sail every morning from both places – In the passage the course of the river is taken, which is beautiful, and in many places picturesque".

"The Liverpool Coaches meet the Packets at the Black Bear Bridge, near Warrington; and there is a Packet at Runcorn, which meets the Navigation Packets for the conveyance of passengers between that place and Liverpool".

The morning boat set off from Runcorn at 10 a.m. in summer, 8 a.m. in winter, arriving at Manchester eight hours later. Through fares ranged from 3s 6d to 2s 3d. The Old Quay's packet wharf at Liverpool was on the west side of George's Dock.

Between 1806 and 1814 the affairs of the Mersey & Irwell Company were in the hands of John Nightingale. He laid down the firm foundation upon which were built many years of prosperity. The year 1819 saw work begin on Woolston New Cut. $1^3/_4$ miles long and opened in 1821, the new cut by-passed a three-mile meandering journey along the winding river loops of the Woolston Eyes. In 1816, steam-driven packet boats were introduced on the estuary between Liverpool and Runcorn. During the 1820s the annual weight of goods passing to and from

Liverpool by water amounted to some 250,000 tons – 85 per cent of which went in the Liverpool-Manchester direction – along either the Mersey & Irwell Navigation or the Bridgewater Canal, in a time of about twelve hours. All this was to change with the coming of the Railway Age.

The Decline of the Mersey & Irwell Company

The Liverpool & Manchester Railway opened in 1830. Much to the railway company's surprise, the infant rail link at first captured only a small fraction of the Liverpool-Manchester goods traffic. Most of the railway's early revenue came from passengers. By 1845 it had managed to take only one-third of the total goods trade.

However, following the death of Thomas Lingard, the Principal Agent of the Mersey & Irwell Navigation, a price war erupted between the old navigation and the Bridgewater Trust. Continual rounds of freight charge cuts eventually brought about the eclipse of the Old Quay Company. By 1843 the navigation was in need of a thorough overhaul for which no finance was available. The company had finally overreached itself and had burnt itself out. On New Year's Day 1844, Lord Francis Egerton offered £400,000 for the Mersey & Irwell shares. They were transferred to the Bridgewater Trust on January 1st 1846. The Old Quay Company no longer existed. Under Bridgewater control, the navigation was badly maintained and was allowed to fall into disrepair.

The Old Navigation and the Manchester Ship Canal

Construction of the Manchester Ship Canal, officially opened by Queen Victoria in May 1894, began in a field on the banks of the Mersey estuary, about three-quarters of a mile upstream of the Ferry Hotel at Eastham, when its first sod was ceremonially cut by Lord Egerton of Tatton. The Ship Canal Company needed the old Mersey & Irwell Navigation as a guiding channel and as a water supply for the new waterway. In order to get its hands on the navigation, the canal company purchased outright, for £1,710,000, all the Bridgewater Navigation Company's assets, including the Bridgewater Canal and all its docks and wharves.

Irish Coaster Rathmoy *with M.S.C. tugs* Valiant *(fore) and* Viking *(aft) passing Ellesmere Port towards Eastham Locks on the Ship Canal (5th July 1993)*

Beyond its locks at Latchford, the ship canal passes beneath the M6 Thelwall viaduct and meets the incoming River Bollin near Rixton before reaching Warburton Bridge. East of Warburton, the canal makes its way along the old course of the Mersey past Cadishead and Partington. On the south bank of the canal, the narrow upper Mersey, having come down from Stockport, flows into the ship canal. Thereafter, the canal's course to Manchester almost completely swallowed up the Irwell section of the Old Quay Company's navigation.

The Mersey & Irwell Navigation did not surrender to the ship canal without a struggle. In January 1890, during the construction of the ship canal, a rapid thaw of lying snow, combined with very heavy rain, caused the old navigation to break through its retaining embankments and flood into the canal's excavations. A similar calamity occurred in February and again in March. The month of November 1890 began with virtually continuous torrential rain. A massive volume of water came down the Mersey, the Irwell and their tributaries, flooding the entire length of the ship canal between Latchford and Trafford Park. Digging machinery, cranes, railway wagons, horse carts and equipment were washed like driftwood down the channel of the canal. To pay for the drainage of the flooded areas and the replacement of plant, the canal company had to borrow £3 million from Manchester Corporation.

The ship canal, having swallowed up some six miles of the course of the Mersey, now obscures the Irwell's course almost completely. A few remnants of the old Irwell are still in view between Rixton and Manchester. A short stretch remains at Irlam and there are small lengths further north at Hulme's Ferry and near Peel Green.

The Leeds & Liverpool Canal

On July 2nd 1766 a public meeting to promote the construction of a canal between Leeds and Liverpool was held at the Sun Inn, Bradford. The promoters planned to make the new canal part of a continuous waterway route between the ports of Hull and Liverpool. (Leeds was already linked to Hull via the Aire & Calder navigation, connecting with the River Humber at Goole).

Following the formation of separate committees at Bradford and Liverpool, the Yorkshire engineer John Longbotham surveyed a route for the canal. His proposed waterway would enter Lancashire at Colne, run down the valleys of the Calder and the Ribble towards Preston, and then through West Lancashire, via Ormskirk and Bootle into Liverpool.

During the month of February 1769, over £40,000 was subscribed at Liverpool in shares to 'The Yorkshire & Lancashire Canal'. A similar amount was paid in at Bradford. Anxious to ensure that the new canal would bring fresh coal supplies into the town, the Liverpool committee, in variance with Longbotham's proposed route, wanted the canal to have access to the Wigan coalfield. Consequently, John Eyes and Richard Melling surveyed a new route on behalf of the Liverpool shareholders.

Liverpool-Wigan Canal Packet (1829)		
	Front Cabin	Back Cabin
Mr Banner's Land	0 6	0 4
Kirkdale Marsh	0 6	0 4
Mr Jackson's Tenement, Bootle	0 8	0 6
Linacre-Brook	0 8	0 6
Ford	0 10	0 6
To the West of Gorsey Lane	1 0	0 6
Buckley-hill	1 0	0 7
Netherton, Jonathan Rigby's	1 0	0 8
Aintree	1 $1^1/_2$	0 9
Alt Valley	1 2	0 10
Melling-road	1 $4^1/_2$	0 11
Melling-brook	1 6	1 0
Red Lion, Maghull	1 $7^1/_2$	1 1
Alty's-bridge, Lydiate	1 9	1 2
Deep-cutting, Lydiate	1 $10^1/_2$	1 3
Smith's-bridge, Lydiate	2 0	1 4
Down Holland-hall	2 $1^1/_2$	1 5
Halsall-hill	2 3	1 6
Halsall-warehouse	2 $4^1/_2$	1 7
Scarisbrick-pinfold	2 6	1 8
Scarisbrick-deep-cutting	2 $7^1/_2$	1 9
Martin-hall-ground	2 9	1 10
Martin-hall-wood	2 $10^1/_2$	1 11
Burscough-bridge	3 0	2 0
Brier's-mill	3 $1^1/_2$	2 1
Thomas Rigby's, Newburgh	3 3	2 2
John Monks	3 $4^1/_2$	2 3
Owler-lane, Parbold	3 6	2 4
Gillibrand's-bridge	3 6	2 5
Appley-warehouse and beyond	3 6	2 6

From *Williamson's Liverpool Advertiser*

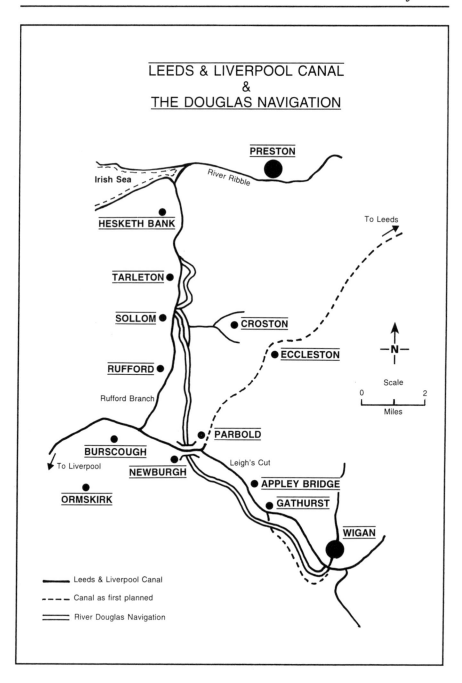

At first the Yorkshire promoters turned down the new plan, but, after the Liverpool faction had protested by withdrawing their subscriptions, a compromise route was agreed. The canal would now be built to connect, via Burnley, Blackburn and Chorley, to a junction with the River Douglas at Newburgh, near Parbold. This arrangement would enable canal boats to come down from Wigan and enter the canal at the junction. A Bill passed smoothly through parliament and became law on May 19th 1770. The title of the 1770 Act states its purpose like this:

"An Act for making and maintaining a Navigable Cut or Canal from Leeds Bridge in the County of York to North Lady's Walk in Liverpoole in the County Palatine of Lancaster, and from thence to the River Mersey".

The Leeds & Liverpool Canal before 1790

Construction was officially started by the ceremonial cutting of the first sod of the Liverpool-Newburgh section by C.L. Morduant at Halsall on February 5th 1771. By the summer of 1772, the canal company, which had purchased control of the Douglas Navigation, was extending the canal towards Wigan. In February 1774 the line had reached Gathurst, where it was connected by Leigh's Cut to the River Douglas at Dean Lock. The ultimate aim was to bypass the Douglas altogether. (See Map).

By October, the canal basin at the Liverpool terminus had been finished. Coal from the Wigan and Orrell pits could now be brought directly to Liverpool. The boats were sailed or man-hauled from Wigan to Gathurst, where they entered the new canal. From Gathurst, they journeyed through Appley Bridge, Parbold, Newburgh, Halsall, Lydiate, Maghull, Aintree and Bootle, before reaching the new wharf at Old Hall Street, a distance of about 31 miles.

This is how *Williamson's Liverpool Advertiser* described the celebrations at the official opening of the Liverpool-Gathurst section in October 1774:

"On Wednesday last, the part of the Leeds Canal between Liverpool and Wigan was opened with great festivity and rejoicings. The water had been let into the basin the day before. At nine, the Proprietors sailed up the canal in their barge, preceded by another filled with music with flying colours etc. and returned about one. They were saluted by two Royal Salutes of twenty-one guns each, besides the swivels on board the boats, and welcomed with the repeated shouts of

the numerous crowds assembled on the banks, who made a most cheerful and agreeable sight. The gentlemen then adjourned to a tent, where a cold collation was provided for them and their friends. From thence they went in procession to Georges Coffee House, where an elegant dinner was provided. The workmen, 215 in number, walked first with their tools on their shoulders and cockades in their hats, and were afterwards regaled of a dinner provided for them. The bells rang all day and the greatest joy and order prevailed on the occasion".

The canal reached Wigan in 1780. A canal branch, $7^3/_4$ miles long, running between Burscough and Rufford towards the Ribble estuary at Tarleton, was opened in 1781. The coal tonnage shipped from the Wigan district increased almost fourfold between 1781 and 1790 to an annual figure of some 160,000 tons. Coal was still carried on the Douglas to join the canal at Gathurst. As increasing proportion went via the canal all the way.

By the 1790s, Leeds & Liverpool Canal coal went chiefly for export. Most of Liverpool's industrial coal came down the Sankey Canal. Household coal continued to come by road from the Prescot pits.

One very durable and long-lived coalmining company, generated by the opening of the Leeds & Liverpool, was that founded by Jonathan Blundell, the fourth son of Bryan Blundell, the slave-trader and privateer who founded the Liverpool Blue Coat School. Trading as 'Samuel Warren and Co.', Blundell and his partners built an enclosed coal yard on land at the north end of Old Hall Street, together with an office and a large private house. Wigan coal was unloaded at a private wharf. In 1766 the company took a lease on the Orrell House colliery and bought it outright in 1780. The Blundell mining company, continued by Jonathan's son Henry, developed into a powerful empire, embracing pits at Ince, Pemberton, Blackrod and Chorley. It continued, as the Pemberton Colliery Company, until the nationalization of the coal industry in 1947.

In 1782 the Leeds & Liverpool Canal Company had used up all its capital. Construction work ground to a halt. Fifty-six miles of the authorized route had yet to be built.

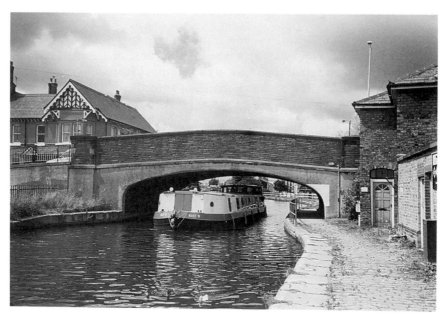

Burscough Bridge

Completion of the Canal

In 1790, eight years after building stopped, following a campaign mounted by company chairman John Hustler, an Act was obtained which allowed the company an extra borrowing power of £200,000 towards the completion work. Work resumed. However, three years later, the company had to get an Act so that it could borrow even more money. A further £280,000 was sanctioned in 1794. The canal was then extended through Burnley and Accrington towards Blackburn under the supervision of surveyor and engineer Robert Whitworth.

By 1796 the summit level of the canal had been carried underground through Foulridge Tunnel. 1,640 yards long, the tunnel took five years to build. At Burnley, Whitworth took the canal over the Calder valley on a 60-feet high embankment three-quarters of a mile long. Beyond Burnley he led it underground through the 560 yards Gannow Tunnel. Whitworth, who died in 1799, was succeeded as Chief Engineer by Samuel Fletcher.

By 1810 the canal consisted of a northern section of length 71 miles between Leeds and Blackburn as well as the Liverpool-Wigan line. Again short of funds, the company made an agreement with the proprietors of the Lancaster Canal, whereby the Leeds & Liverpool was to link up with an eleven-mile section of the Lancaster, bringing itself to a point just east of Wigan. A flight of 21 locks was built to carry the canal 200 feet up from the centre of Wigan to a junction with the Lancaster at Wigan Top Lock. Following the completion of a final short section south of Blackburn, the completed trans-Pennine waterway opened to through traffic on October 23rd 1816 – fifty years after the initial meeting at The Sun. To mark the occasion, a decorated fleet of boats set off from Leeds. Four days later, after a multitude of celebrations along the way, the procession arrived in triumph at Liverpool to an official reception.

It had taken 46 years to build the canal, covering $127^1/_4$ miles between the Aire Bridge at Leeds and Old Hall Street, Liverpool.

The Leeds & Liverpool Canal (1816-1870)

Throughout its history the canal carried very little through traffic. Apart from the Wigan-Liverpool coal trade, raw cotton landed at Liverpool was taken for spinning to mills at Blackburn, Accrington, Burnley and other Lancashire towns. The carrying was at first done by private companies and independent boatmen who paid the canal company a tonnage charge. As well as general merchandise, the Leeds & Liverpool, like most waterways, carried large quantities of bulky materials like limestone and bricks: road carriage would have time-consuming and expensive. The cargo side of the business, which first broke even in 1786, continued to remain profitable until as late as 1919.

Passenger boats, in operation since the 1770s, continued until 1848, when the railways had become quicker and more convenient. The Leeds & Liverpool used to run a passenger service to and from Liverpool and Wigan, and also a local service between Liverpool and Aintree Vale. Three boats a day ran from Liverpool through Bootle to Linacre Brook, where a coach took passengers on to Crosby. Fares for the 1829 Wigan service, based upon places corresponding to successive mile stones, worked out at about $1^1/_2$d per mile (front cabin) and 1d per mile (back cabin). (See Fare Table).

Although a Liverpool-Wigan rail link opened in 1832, the railway was not equipped to handle vast quantities of coal. In 1833, half a million tons came into Liverpool altogether; the Leeds & Liverpool handled half of the amount. In the 1830s, in order to combat railway competition, the Leeds & Liverpool carriers used a fleet of 'fly-boats' providing an express service, mainly for lighter cargoes, operating to a strict timetable. These boats were hauled by relays of horses, changed frequently to obtain maximum speed.

By 1845, cargo once carried on the canal began to be taken by rail. This was the year of the company's highest toll revenue. Thereafter, although the company continued to make a profit, its annual income began to fall.

A report of 1843 showed that of 1,375,000 tons of British-made goods passing through Liverpool, 252,000 tons arrived on the Leeds & Liverpool Canal. This figure compares with 370,000 tons via the Bridgewater Canal and 340,000 tons via the Mersey & Irwell Navigation. The weight of goods arriving at the two railway termini at Park Lane and Crown Street was reported as 250,000 tons in total.

In August 1848, after a period of expansion of the north docks by the Liverpool Dock Trustees, the canal was at last connected to the Mersey. Four locks led vessels down a 400-yard branch into Stanley Dock.

In August 1850, when railway competition was starting to bite, the canal company made a deal with a consortium of railway-owned carrying companies whereby, for an annual rent of £40,000, the lessees would collect the cargo tolls on the lighter general goods, leaving the Leeds & Liverpool Company to carry bulky cargoes like coal, metals, ores and bricks.

By mid-century, because of competition from the growing rail network, canal companies began to amalgamate. Some drained their canals and built railways along them, making use of ready-made embankments and cuttings. To survive, a canal company had to modernize its waterway, docks and warehouses, as well as improving the efficiency of its carrying service. In the 1850s the Leeds & Liverpool Company widened the Liverpool end of the canal to take larger craft. After 1870, steam barges, most of them pulling several 'dumb' barges behind them, were in use. Steam haulage was first introduced on the long level section between Liverpool and Appley Bridge.

Progress of the Leeds & Liverpool Canal after 1870

The last quarter of the 1800s saw the canal hold on to its traffic despite a period of intense rivalry from the railways. It was only after 1890 that profits began to tumble. After 1918, both traffic and profits fell away rapidly. The canal company would have liked to have deepened and widened the waterway so that it could accommodate the large modern steamships. Unfortunately, the engineering problems in such a scheme were immense. Enlargement of the water channel was in many places impossible, particularly in towns where the canal passed through confined spaces or over and under road and rail bridges.

By 1900 very little traffic covered the whole length of the canal. In 1905, out of a total tonnage of about 2 million tons, (1.2 million of which was coal), only 13,000 tons was through traffic: 8,000 tons went from Liverpool to Leeds and 5,000 tons in the opposite direction.

After 1900 the company rarely paid its shareholders a dividend. The company's position worsened after the 1914-1918 war, when a glut of ex-army lorries began to carry goods. In 1921 its barges and steam tugs were sold off. Operating as 'Canal Transport Ltd', the canal company continued to move cargo and made small annual profits until the outbreak of the Second World War in 1939.

Large losses were incurred in the immediate post-war years. Nationalization came in 1948 and the Liverpool canal basins were filled in. The Liverpool terminal moved to Chisenhale Street in 1960. This was the year in which the last commercial cargo was carried between Lancashire and Yorkshire. Coal from Wigan was carried to Liverpool's Athol Street gas works until 1964.

The Leeds & Liverpool Canal, expensive to maintain, has been kept navigable throughout its length as a cruiseway for pleasure craft. Boating, based at numerous marinas, remains popular. The canal is vitally important for land drainage. Between Liverpool and Old Roan, surface water drains into the canal at no fewer than two hundred places. In the later 1980s a five-mile stretch between Liverpool and Aintree was landscaped. The improvement, financed by the Merseyside Development Corporation in conjunction with the electricity supply industry, was part of a national drive to open up and improve canal towing paths and to strengthen the role of the canal as a leisure amenity.

Wigan Pier Museum and the Orwell Restaurant

The Bridgewater Canal

The Duke of Bridgewater's canal begins at Worsley, about four miles north-west of Manchester, near Junction 13 of the M62 motorway. It then runs into Manchester through Barton-upon-Irwell where it is carried across the Manchester Ship Canal by the Barton Aqueduct. Just before the Bridgewater reaches the Warrington-Manchester railway line, its course divides. One branch goes to Manchester; the main line continues southwestwards to cross the upper Mersey at Barfoot Bridge. After passing through Sale and Altrincham, the canal runs along a high embankment past Dunham Hall, then through Lymm and Grappenhall, past Stockton Heath and through the Cheshire countryside via Walton and Moore to Preston Brook where it connects with the Trent & Mersey Canal. The Bridgewater then doubles back, past the ruins of Norton Priory into Runcorn, just beyond the Victoria Bridge. Here a flight of locks used to lead the canal down into the Mersey estuary. (There is also a short line from Worsley to Leigh). (See map on page 000).

In 1758 the 22-year-old Francis Egerton, 3rd Duke of Bridgewater, directed John Gilbert, his personal agent and chief engineer at his coal pits on Walkden Moor, to draw up a plan for a canal from the Egerton estate at Worsley into Salford. The idea was to cheapen the cost of carrying the Duke's coal into Salford and Manchester. In March 1759 the Duke obtained the necessary Act of Parliament and construction work began under John Gilbert's supervision.

By the end of 1759 the Duke had changed his mind about the route of his canal. On the advice of consultant engineer James Brindley, the new plan was to carry the canal across the River Irwell by means of an aqueduct at Barton. Having crossed the Irwell, the canal would then run along the south side of the river to terminate in Manchester rather than in Salford.

In January 1760, James Brindley, giving evidence to a parliamentary committee, laid on a convincing practical demonstration of how the Duke's canal – the first British canal of any great length – would be made completely and safely watertight. The method involved lining the canal with 'clay-puddle' (clay saturated with water). In front of the penetrating gaze of the committee, Brindley moulded a flat narrow vessel out of the material, poured water into it, and established to everyone's satisfaction that the clay-puddle was impermeable.

An Act enabling a change of route was passed in March 1760. The scale and originality of Brindley's engineering work on the Bridgewater was, in the 1700s, epoch-making, a significant breakthrough in civil engineering. To avoid the necessity for locks, the canal was built on a single level throughout its length. High embankments and deep cuttings, now commonplace on road and rail journeys, were then a fairly new idea on

Britain. The Duke's canal was destined to be the forerunner of a whole host of canals, as well as providing a reservoir of knowledge upon which the railway pioneers were to draw in the next century.

No sooner had the Duke obtained the second Act than he was seeking a third. His idea was to extend his canal to the Mersey estuary. The aim was to capture Liverpool-Manchester traffic from the Mersey & Irwell Navigation. The enabling Act received the royal assent in March 1762.

In 1765 the Duke opened his wharf at Castlefield in Manchester. By June 1766 the canal had reached Altrincham and by 1769, Lymm. In 1771 the line of the canal was complete, apart from a disputed section across Sir Richard Brooke's estate at Norton. 1773 saw the opening of a ten-lock flight down a 90-ft hill into the Mersey at Runcorn. The Bridgewater, connected to a new Trent & Mersey Canal at Preston Brook in 1775, was opened to through traffic on March 21st 1776, giving a Runcorn-Manchester distance of 28 miles.

Worsley coal was being sold at Liverpool as early as 1774. **Williamson's Liverpool Advertiser** hailed the Duke as a public benefactor:

" We cannot do greater Honor to his Grace the Duke of Bridgewater, than by telling to the World that, he is selling at Liverpool, a single Pennyworth of Coals to everyone who chuses to purchase. For this humane act the prayers of the Poor shall proclaim him their Benefactor. He sells Twenty-Four Pound of Coal for the Penny, and if it was not for the unfortunate Obstruction in Cheshire, which prevents the completion of his canal, he would sell them to the Poor even cheaper than that".

The Bridgewater Canal (1776-1803)

The opening of the Trent & Mersey Canal in 1777 allowed an immense quantity of cargo to pass to and from the Bridgewater Canal at Preston Brook. It was here that goods were transhipped between the narrow Trent & Mersey boats and the broad esturial sailing flats used on the Bridgewater.

Coal traffic on the canal was outweighed in total by other commodities like cotton, pottery, timber, grain, limestone, iron ore and agricultural produce. By 1791 the Duke had a fleet of his own sailing flats. The

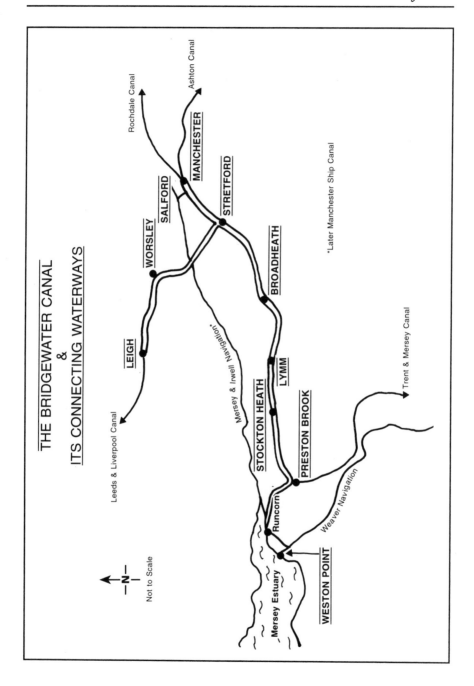

THE BRIDGEWATER CANAL
&
ITS CONNECTING WATERWAYS

Not to Scale

Rochdale Canal

Ashton Canal

MANCHESTER

STRETFORD

SALFORD

WORSLEY

LEIGH

BROADHEATH

*Later Manchester Ship Canal

Mersey & Irwell Navigation*

Leeds & Liverpool Canal

STOCKTON HEATH

LYMM

PRESTON BROOK

Trent & Mersey Canal

Weaver Navigation

Runcorn

Mersey Estuary

WESTON POINT

N

annual tonnage had risen to over 250,000 by 1791. Of this total, 83,000 tons was moved from Liverpool, of which 19,000 tons was transhipped down the Trent & Mersey at Preston Brook. Some 30,000 tons arrived at Liverpool, 20,000 of it from the Staffordshire potteries via the Trent & Mersey Canal. Liverpool supplied goods from the United States and the West Indies like cotton, sugar and tobacco, china clay for the Staffordshire potters, wool and linen from Ireland. These commodities travelled via Preston Brook. Almost a third of the traffic arriving on the Bridgewater at the Duke's Dock in Liverpool was rock salt, carried down the Trent & Mersey Canal from the Cheshire mines. Because the Bridgewater connected with the Trent & Mersey, it had access to the ports of Hull and Bristol, as well as with Staffordshire, Birmingham and the Midlands.

Passenger services, at first horse-drawn and later steam-hauled, were introduced in 1767. The slowness of the packet boats (3 m.p.h.) was counterbalanced by comfort and reliability. They were to operate until 1868, by when the railways had rendered them obsolete.

The Bridgewater Trust

Francis, 3rd Duke of Bridgewater, died on March 8th 1803. The canal had been his personal property. To finance it, a debt of £340,000 in 1789 was to be cleared only after the Duke's death. Under the terms of the will, a trust was set up to administer the estate. The will laid down that the trust had to remain in existence until the deaths of all the peers in the House of Lords and of their sons, followed by an additional period of twenty-one years. (The trust lasted for a hundred years, until 1903).

The Duke's will gave virtual dictatorial powers to his canal manager Robert Haldane Bradshaw. He was given these powers for life, together with the free use of Worsley Hall and Bridgewater House at Runcorn.

In 1821 the Bridgewater was connected to Leigh to the Leeds & Liverpool Canal, giving the latter access to Manchester. Cargo tonnages increased markedly from 490,000 tons in 1820 to 730,000 tons in 1825. A programme of new locks and improved docks at Runcorn was complete by 1828.

The 1840s were boom years for the Bridgewater Canal. Under the guidance of James Loch and Lord Ellesmere, the Trust managed to handle successfully the competition both from the railways and from its rival waterway, the Mersey & Irwell Navigation. The cargo figure for 1845 was 1,391,000 tons. The following year saw the Trust purchase the near-bankrupt Mersey & Irwell Company.

Trade declined after 1846. Railway companies began to amalgamate with each other and with canal companies. The Bridgewater became virtually surrounded by waterways under railway control. Meanwhile, the Trust soldiered on alone.

Under the superintendence of Algernon Egerton, the trustees had a duty to ensure that the Egerton family received a steady income. Consequently, in 1872, the Trust's canal assets were transferred to a new company involving the Manchester, Sheffield & Lincolnshire Railway and the Midland Railway. It was called the Bridgewater Navigation Company. The assets transferred were the Bridgewater Canal, the rundown Mersey & Irwell Navigation, docks and warehouses at Liverpool, Manchester and Runcorn and a sizeable fleet of barges.

Before the Ship Canal

Under the management of Edward Leader Williams, the Bridgewater Navigation Company launched a programme of thorough modernization. The canal's depth was increased from 4ft 6in to 6 feet. A new dock, the Fenton, was built at Runcorn. In 1876 a fleet of 26 new steam tugs, each capable of hauling four laden dumb barges, came into use.

The Canal under Ship Canal Control

So that it could take possession of the Mersey & Irwell Navigation and use it as a foundation and water supply for the new giant waterway, the Manchester Ship Canal Company purchased the Bridgewater Canal as well. It then operated separately from the ship canal as the 'Bridgewater Department' of the parent company.

Because traffic was transferred to the ship canal, Bridgewater tonnages began to fall after 1885. In 1888, 2,447,000 tons were carried. The 1898 figure was 1,919,000 tons; that for 1905 was 1,867,000 tons.

Bridgewater through traffic between Liverpool and Manchester – chiefly cotton, timber, grain and sugar – continued to flourish. 'Down' traffic for export included iron, machinery and finished cotton goods. By 1907 all the Bridgewater Department's barges were steam-hauled. There were 238 barges and 22 narrow boats. However, private 'by-traders' accounted for as much as two-thirds of the total tonnage. The Duke's Dock in Liverpool was sold to the Mersey Docks and Harbour Board in 1900 for £522,000 and the Department continued to use it on a lease.

The Twentieth Century

Although traffic on the Bridgewater fell after the First World War, forcing the Ship Canal Company to give up its tenancy of the Liverpool dock in 1921, business perked up a little after the Second War. In 1947 the canal was deepened to accommodate the big barges carrying grain to the Kellogg factory at Trafford park. However, raw materials to the Potteries started to be moved by road. All barge traffic at Liverpool ceased in 1947.

In 1960, with the new Widnes-Runcorn bridge under construction, linked to a growing motorway network, the Ship Canal Company disposed of the flight of locks at Runcorn, the dock-canal connection there, and the Runcorn & Weston Canal. A new lock was built to connect the Runcorn docks directly to the ship canal, giving them a new lease of life.

The last cargoes on the Bridgewater included coal supplies to Stretford Gas Works and to Barton Power Station. Until 1972, coal was moved from Leigh through Worsley to feed the power station at Trafford Park.

In 1973 the Bridgewater Department was converted into a road haulage business with headquarters near the old Castlefield wharves in Manchester. The barge fleet was sold off in 1974.

The Bridgewater Canal is today a quiet waterway running through Cheshire to Runcorn, with a branch line to Worsley and to Leigh. Since 1974 it has been controlled by a trust made up of representatives of the M.S.C. Company and local government.

The Bridgewater has proved to be a valuable amenity for the communities through which it passes. As well as providing excellent facilities for boating and angling, the towpath is accessible to walkers throughout its length. The canal is far from being run-down legacy from our industrial past. It is a public leisure amenity of the highest order, a worthy memorial of the Canal Age.

The Shropshire Union Canal

The first component of the Shropshire Union Canal network was the Chester Canal. Running from the River Dee at Chester to Nantwich, a distance of nineteen miles, it was completed in 1779.

The idea behind the Chester Canal was to draw Cheshire salt and Midlands pottery cargoes towards Chester and away from Liverpool. it had been hoped that the canal could be built to connect with the Trent & Mersey Canal at Middlewich, but the enabling Act disallowed a junction. The Chester Canal Company, in a desperate attempt to get traffic on to its ailing waterway, carried out a search for rock salt at Nantwich but found none. All efforts to attract traffic ended in failure.

John Aikin, writing in 1795, did not beat around the bush about the shortcomings of the Chester Canal:

"For want of money, the branch to Middlewich was never cut; and thus the principal objects of the undertaking, the carriage of salt from that place to Chester being never effected, the scheme has proved more totally abortive than any other in the kingdom".

The Wirral Line

The Chester Canal was saved from oblivion in 1797 by being joined to the Wirral Line of the Ellesmere Canal. A canal to link the Mersey to the Dee was launched at a meeting at Ellesmere in Shropshire in August 1791. A group of men with interests in the industrial area around Wrexham were seeking an outlet to the Mersey for their products. They also planned a waterway connection to the Severn at Shrewsbury.

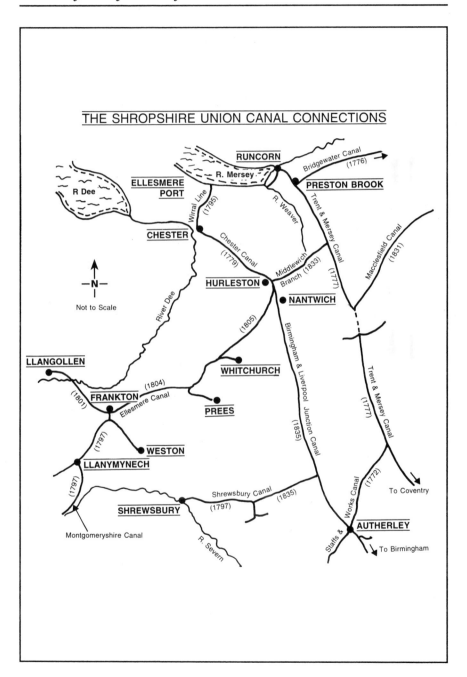

THE SHROPSHIRE UNION CANAL CONNECTIONS

Work on the Wirral Line, part of a projected Mersey-Chester-Shrewsbury waterway, began in November 1793 and was completed within two years. Running for $8^3/4$ miles between Chester and 'Whitby Locks' (later known as Ellesmere Port), the Wirral Line of the Ellesmere Canal was welcomed by the Corporation and citizens of Chester as a new transport route to supplement the Chester-Birkenhead turnpike and their traditional waterway, the River Dee.

The Wirral Line was an immediate success. Its profits helped to pay for the building of the rest of the Ellesmere Canal. The waterway was cut across the Wirral without the need for locks. To keep a level line, the canal was led through the narrow valley of the Backford Gap, thereby avoiding numerous sandstone ridges and valleys. The line connected with the Mersey estuary at Whitby. (Although the canal company immediately named its new Mersey terminal 'Ellesmere Port', the new name did not come into general use until the 1860s).

Unlike the rest of Ellesmere Canal, the Wirral Line was built as a broad waterway, fourteen feet wide. It could accommodate the flat-bottomed barges which plied to and fro across the Mersey estuary and along the other Mersey waterways. The line was watered from the Mersey itself by the use of a steam pump and by taking water from the Chester Canal at Chester.

In the early years, the Wirral Line got a large proportion of its profits from passenger services. Travellers to and from Liverpool and Chester changed boats at Ellesmere Port. During the summer months, special day trips were laid on to exploit Ellesmere Port's growing popularity as a seaside bathing resort.

By 1796 the Chester Canal company was anxious to revive its ailing waterway by connecting it to the Wirral Line. Eventually, in desperation, the company cut off the Wirral Line's water supply at Chester, forcing the Ellesmere company to agree to a connection. An Ellesmere connection at Chester in 1797 was followed in 1805 by an eastern link at Hurleston. Water was supplied along a feeder canal from the Dee near Llangollen.

Amalgamation and Progress

In 1813 the two companies came together as 'The United Company of Proprietors of the Ellesmere and Chester Canals'. After 1820, while the passenger services on the Wirral Line continued to flourish, goods traffic through Ellesmere Port increased steadily. In 1826 an Act was passed for a canal which revitalized the fortunes of the Ellesmere and Chester Canal and spurred on the growth of Ellesmere Port. This was the Birmingham and Liverpool Junction Canal. It provided a new line from the Midlands to Liverpool, via the Chester Canal at Nantwich, the Wirral Line and Ellesmere Port. The new canal, opened in 1835, was given access to Manchester in 1833 via a branch from the Chester Canal at Barbridge to the Trent & Mersey at Middlewich. (See Map).

The Birmingham & Liverpool Junction Canal allowed cargoes heading for Liverpool from the Midlands to be brought through Chester and Ellesmere Port. They no longer had to be taken via Preston brook and Runcorn on the Bridgewater. Moreover, the journey length was nineteen miles shorter. The increased traffic fuelled the rapid growth of Ellesmere Port.

The Pressure of Competition

In 1840 the staple cargo through Ellesmere Port was iron ore brought down the coast from Whitehaven. The ore was shipped up the Ellesmere to the smelters in the Wrexham area and in Staffordshire. Finished iron was stored and exported from Ellesmere Port.

Successive bouts of price cutting between the Ellesmere & Chester Company and the Bridgewater Trustees, targeted upon the Midlands-Liverpool traffic, weakened the Ellesmere & Chester's finances. Consequently, in 1844 it leased out the carriage of cargoes between Ellesmere Port and Liverpool to the Trustees in return for an annual rental of £4,000.

After 1837 the Wirral Line had to compete with the newly-opened Grand Junction Railway which joined Liverpool to Birmingham. To combat the railway, the Ellesmere & Chester Company and the B.L. & J. Canal ran their affairs in tandem. While many individuals had shares in both companies, the two boards of directors had the same chairman.

The Shropshire Union under Railway Control

In the summer of 1845, 'railway mania' was at its height. Over one hundred new railway companies were formed that year. Not to be left out, the Ellesmere & Chester Company founded, in 1846, a company to build a railway between Wolverhampton and Chester, using the old Birmingham & Liverpool Junction Canal line. The new company was called 'The Shropshire Union Railway and Canal Company'. However, the powerful London & North Western Railway consortium (L.N.W.R.) stepped in and took over the Shropshire Union. (It was to be owned by the L.N.W.R. until the regrouping of the railway network in 1922).

During the period 1875 to 1900 the chief commodities passing through Ellesmere Port were iron ore and iron to and from Staffordshire and Wrexham; flints, clay and finished goods to and from the Potteries; coal for export as back cargo for the outgoing iron ore coasters and general merchandise between Birmingham, Chester and Liverpool.

The Shropshire Union after 1890

In the summer of 1881 the first vessels passed through the entrance locks of the new Manchester Ship Canal at Eastham and made their way to Ellesmere Port. In the twenty years after 1892 the Shropshire Union embarked on a large scale investment programme at Ellesmere Port. New docks, warehouses and a rail connection to the Hooton-Helsby railway were built. The Shropshire Union canal network, leased from the L.N.W.R., had a total length of 200 miles, most of which passed through sparsely-populated countryside. Cargoes, mostly carried in the company's own vessels, became steam-hauled. However, even in 1907, most of the network – apart from the Wirral Line – still relied on horse towage. A cargo tonnage of 370,000 in 1898 increased to 470,000 by 1905.

Because of the high maintenance costs on its long canal network, the Shropshire Union never made large profits. During and after the First World War, its losses increased to alarming levels. In 1921, following the withdrawal of the government's wartime subsidy, an annual loss of £80,000 was recorded. The carriage of cargo in the company's own vessels ceased. Next year, 1922 the Ellesmere Port estate was leased to the Manchester Ship Canal Company. The Shropshire Union, along with the L.N.W.R., was absorbed into the new London Midland & Scottish Railway Company (L.M.S.).

During the inter-war years, while the dock estate at Ellesmere Port was being converted into an oil-based centre, the Shropshire Union Canal entered its final period of decline. A tonnage of 433,000 in 1929 had fallen to 151,000 by 1940. In 1944 a wholesale abandonment occurred. The only parts retained were the main line and the Middlewich Branch, together with the Hurleston-Llangollen line. The latter was kept as a supply channel, feeding water from the River Dee into a reservoir of household water at Hurleston. The canal carried its last cargoes from Ellesmere Port to the Midlands in 1958. Local commercial traffic to and from Chester along the Wirral Line ended in the early 1960s.

The 'Shroppie' is today one of the most popular cruising waterways in the north-west. The section between Hurleston and Llangollen is particularly beautiful. Thronged with boaters in the summer, the Shropshire Union, with its connections to other cruiseways, attracts enthusiasts from a wide area. Its success into a new millenium seems assured.

Wigan Top Lock and the junction with the old line of the Lancaster Canal

The Walks

This section is a collection of rambles along the many rivers and canals which flow into the River Mersey. Walks near Liverpool Bay and by the River Dee have also been included. The routes include journeys along public footpaths and lanes allowing the reader to explore the countryside near the waterways.

The rambles start and finish within or near the Merseyside Transport Area. Public transport information is provided in the following section.

The route of each walk is accompanied by a sketch map. Places of interest, printed in **bold type**, relate to descriptions printed after the route guides.

PUBLIC TRANSPORT INFORMATION

ACTON BRIDGE	British Rail from Liverpool (Lime St.) (not Sundays)
BACKFORD	Crosville Bus to Birkenhead (Woodside)
BLACKBROOK	Manchester Transport (320) from Liverpool (Wigan bus)
BURSCOUGH JUNCTION	Merseyrail from Liverpool (Central) to Ormskirk **then** British Rail (Preston train)
CHESTER	Mersey Rail via Hooton
DOWNHOLLAND	North-Western bus (Liverpool-Southport)
EARLESTOWN	Merseyrail from Liverpool (Lime St.)

ELLESMERE PORT	Merseyrail from Liverpool (Central) to Hooton **then** British Rail (Helsby train)
GARSTON	Merseybus to Speke Road, **or** Merseyrail from Liverpool (Central) (Hunts Cross train)
HALE	Crosville bus to Liverpool
HESWALL	Crosville bus to Birkenhead (Woodside)
HOYLAKE	Merseyrail from Liverpool (Central) (West Kirby train)
LYDIATE	North-Western bus (Liverpool-Southport)
MAGHULL	Merseyrail from Liverpool (Central) (Ormskirk train)
MARTINSCROFT	Warrington Transport
MORETON	Merseyrail to Liverpool (Central)
OLD ROAN	Merseyrail from Liverpool (Central) (Ormskirk train)
PARBOLD	Merseyrail from Liverpool (Central) to Ormskirk **then** bus from Ormskirk bus station
PRESTON BROOK	Crosville bus to Runcorn Old Town Bus Station **then** Crosville bus to Liverpool
RUFFORD	Merseyrail from Liverpool (Central) to Ormskirk **then** British Rail (Preston train)
RUNCORN	Crosville bus from Liverpool to Runcorn Old Town bus station
SANKEY BRIDGES	Crosville bus from Liverpool (Warrington bus)
WARRINGTON	British Rail from Liverpool Lime St.
WEST KIRBY	Merseyrail from Liverpool (Central)
WHELLEY	G.M. Buses into Wigan town centre
WIDNES WEST BANK	North - Western Bus H26
WIGAN	British Rail from Liverpool Lime St.

1. GARSTON – OGLET – DUNGEON POINT – HALE

A walk along the shore of the Mersey Estuary

Distance: 8 miles

Allow: 4 hours

Start: Garston (O.S. Ref: SJ 403844)

Begin the walk in **Garston**, at the junction of St Mary's Road and Speke Road. Walk along Church Road and pass beneath the railway bridge. Cross to the left side and pass **St. Michael's church.** Follow the churchyard wall as it curves to the left into Banks Road.

Walk down the whole length of this road to the junction with Banks Lane. From this point the airport buildings at Speke can be seen over to the left. Turn right, into Windfield Road.

Walk down this road towards the small factories. At the end of the road, pass through a gap into Brunswick Street. Cross the road and go forward along a path on the left side. This path runs down the edge of the industrial estate and leads to the river front.

There is a view across the estuary to the Wirral shore. To the right are the chimneys of Bromborough power station. Then, moving left, the wooded area of Eastham; the oil containers near the Queen Elizabeth II dock; the grassy banks of ship canal dredgings known as Mount Manisty; Ellesmere Port; Stanlow refinery with its tall narrow chimneys, some of them spouting flames; Ince power station; and on the far left, the hills at Helsby and Frodsham.

Follow the path towards Hale. It begins by going through a landscaped area and continues as a broad path. The bricked path soon runs away to the left. Here, continue forward to follow the grassy path along the bank top, between two areas of bracken.

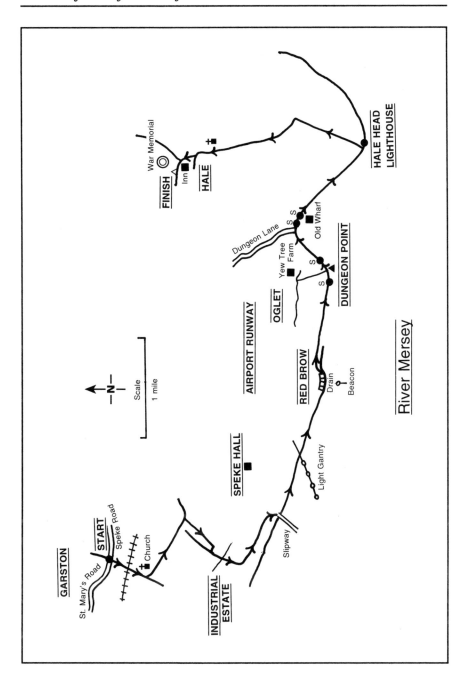

The **airport** comes into view on the far left. The wooded area on the left surrounds **Speke Hall**. It is planned to lay an improved path between Garston and Hale, as part of the Mersey Way path. At the time of writing the path had not yet been completed. Part of the bank further on had collapsed. While the path is incomplete, it is recommended that the walker continues along the sand and shingle for part of the journey.

After a while, follow the path down a concrete ramp to the beach. A long slipway goes out into the river near this point.

Walk along the beach above the high-water line towards a gantry of lights built to assist aircraft as they approach the airport. There are large areas of salt marshes close to the shore. The banks have an abundance of wild plants and the shore is host to a wide variety of wading birds.

Walk towards an old wooden beacon ahead, at the Red Brow. The beacon measures the height of water and stands on an old pile of boulders. Opposite the beacon, walk off the beach up a path on the right of a drain outfall. Go up to the right and continue along the rough track on the bank top, along the boundary of the field.

A scattering of houses at **Oglet** comes into view on the left. The path narrows. Continue along the field edges. The buildings of Yew Tree Farm appear on the left. The farm stands directly opposite Dungeon Point, market by an old light buoy on the shore. Look on the shorelines ahead for the lighthouse at Hale Head.

Pass **Dungeon Point** by going down a flight of wooden steps and climbing up on the opposite side of a track. From this point, an improved pathway leads along the bank to Hale.

The edge of the housing estate at Speke comes into view. It lies beyond the main long airport runway. The shoreline ahead curves away to the **lighthouse**. The path runs parallel to Oglet Lane to reach a car park at the bottom of Dungeon Lane. Pass through the car park and go down the steps.

The journey can be continued along the bank top by climbing the flight of steps. An alternative route is available along the shore, depending on the state of the tide.

On the shore, to the right, just beyond Dungeon Lane, are the remains of an old wharf. This may have been connected with the Dungeon Salt Works in the 1700s, or perhaps with the shrimping boats which used to operate in the locality in the last century.

As the lighthouse is approached, two areas of woodland come into view. The first is known as the Old Plantation. The second is the Ice House Plantation in Hale Park. These trees used to screen off **Hale Hall**. At low tide large sandbanks in the estuary can be seen. The extreme narrowness of the river channel is then in evidence.

When the lighthouse has been reached, leave the shore by walking up the narrow lane towards Hale village. The course of the Mersey changes direction sharply at Hale Head. On the opposite side of the Mersey can be seen the high ground at Helsby and Frodsham. A little further upstream the River Weaver spills over from the Manchester Ship Canal through the Weaver Sluices. The factories over at Runcorn are in view. As you walk up the lane, the top of the Widnes-Runcorn road bridge can be seen between two small copses in the field to the right.

After some 600 yards, you reach a road. This leads through the village. It passes **St Mary's church** and the **Childe of Hale Inn**. Buses for Liverpool stop just beyond the inn, opposite the war memorial.

Garston

Garston was not taken into the city of Liverpool until 1902. The old township of Garston used to extend from Speke Road to the boundary with the township of Toxteth Park at Aigburth Vale. In the early years Garston was a fishing village. Many of the fishermen lived on an island off-shore. The shore was later filled in and a sea wall built, which enclosed the island.

Garston today is a container terminal which deals with a large amount of shipping. As early as 1798 a small dock was built to accommodate vessels visiting Blackburne's Salt Works. Rock salt continued to be refined at Garston until 1865. The Garston docks are 'Old' (1846), 'North' (1867), and 'Stalbridge' (1909).

St Michael's Church

The first church on the site was built in 1225. In 1715 it was replaced by a new building which was paid for by Edward Norris of Speke Hall. The present building was opened in 1877. The two churches stood side by side until 1888, when Norris's building was demolished. Stone from the old church was used to build the churchyard wall.

Speke Airport

The airport is built on land bought by Liverpool Corporation from the Speke Hall estate in 1928. It was opened in 1932. A farmhouse was converted for use as a control building in the early years. The first regular service was run between Liverpool and Croydon by Imperial Airways, with calls at Manchester and Birmingham. The airport was put into use by the air force in the Second World War. When jet aircraft began to be used for civil flights the airport was extended by the construction of a 7,500 ft runway.

Speke Hall

The hall dates from 1467. For centuries it was the manor house of Speke and the home of the Norris family. The hall is leased by Liverpool Corporation to the National Trust. It is today surrounded by the airport and the modern town. Land from the estate was bought by the corporation in 1929 and in 1937 work began on the construction of a large town with a large industrial estate. The area along the Mersey at Oglet and Hale was retained as a green belt.

Oglet

This tiny hamlet today consists of only a few dwellings. In the last century it was a village which housed folk engaged in shrimp trawling. The shrimps were carried in large baskets balanced on the heads of the fishermen's wives and daughters and carried from Oglet to Garston market.

Dungeon

The name 'dungeon' has been used to describe a narrow creek surrounded by trees on sloping ground. Two other walks in this book include the name – at Heswall and at Croughton in Cheshire.

In 1697 Thomas Johnson set up a salt refinery at Dungeon Point. Rock salt from the Northwich area was carried overland to Frodsham, where it was loaded on to boats and taken down the River Weaver and across the Mersey to the refinery. Coal used for the boiling of the salt was carried from the mines around Prescot.

Hale Lighthouse

The lighthouse stands upon a sandstone rock at Hale Head. The first house was built in 1836. The present building dates from 1906. It continued in use until 1958 before being converted into a private dwelling house.

Hale Lighthouse

Hale

The manor of Hale was owned by the Ireland family for many generations. Sir Gilbert Ireland built Hale Hall in the 1620s. The building has recently been demolished. The hall's grounds and gardens are now used as a public park.

St Mary's Church

A church was built on the site in the 1300s. The tower dates back to that time. The church was rebuilt in 1758. In 1977 the interior and roof were destroyed by a fire lit by a youth from Speke.

The churchyard is the burial place of John Middleton, a giant known as the Childe of Hale. His tomb is railed off on the right side of the building.

The Childe of Hale

John Middleton was born in Hale, probably in 1573. He is reputed to have been 9ft 3in tall. He was employed by Sir Gilbert Ireland of Hale Hall as his bodyguard. When James I got to hear about Middleton he asked Ireland to take him down to the court in London. Middleton was on show there for a year or more before returning to Hale, where he remained until his death in 1623.

2. HOYLAKE – MEOLS – NORTH WIRRAL COASTAL PARK – LEASTOWE – LIGHTHOUSE – MORETON

A walk along the Wirral coastline between the estuaries of the Mersey and the Dee

Distance: 4¹/₂ miles

Allow: 2 hours

Start: Hoylake Railway Station (O.S. Ref: SJ 217888)

On emerging from Hoylake railway station, walk up Station Road. Bear right, and then go left along Queen's Road. Cross the main road and continue to the bottom of Queen's Road. Walk to the left along Marine Road. The first turning to the right leads to the **Hoylake promenade.**

The promenade directly overlooks Liverpool Bay. To the left, **Hilbre Island** is in view. In the distance, across the estuary of the River Dee, is the coast of North Wales.

There is a continuous coastal pathway between Hoylake and Seacombe, a distance of some ten miles. In recent years, access has been allowed to the river-front beyond Seacombe, towards Birkenhead Docks. Our journey will follow the first few miles of the coastline.

Begin by turning right and walking in the direction of Meols. About 200 yards along is the Hoylake Lifeboat Station. A slipway runs down from the promenade to the shore directly opposite the building. next to the lifeboat station is a boatyard for small vessels. The promenade is fronted by large villas set back from the road.

A grassed section is reached, with a paddling pool jutting out from the promenade. This is the site of the old Hoylake open-air swimming pool, now demolished. The ornamental drinking fountain is an interesting piece of Victoriana.

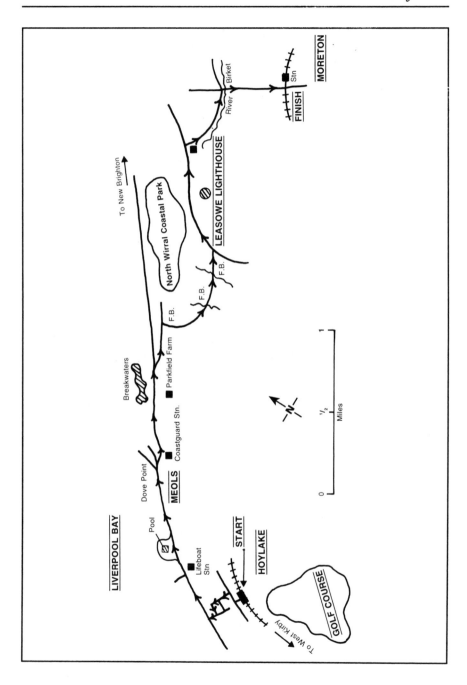

The promenade veers slightly to the left and continues. About a mile further on is Dove Point Slipway at **Meols**. Fishing boats set off and land here regularly. When the catch is sufficient, fish is sold from wagons on the promenade.

Just beyond the slipway, leave the promenade, and walk along to the end of the road. Continue forward along the sandy path which runs above the top of the sea wall. The path passes in front of the Coastguard Station. Keep near the top of the wall.

Inland, just to the right, is Parkfield Farm. **Leasowe Lighthouse** comes into view ahead. Beyond the lighthouse, a little to the right, you can see the tall buildings in Birkenhead and Liverpool. The distant shoreline on the horizon ahead is the coastal area north of Liverpool, leading out past Seaforth and Crosby to Formby Point.

Victorian drinking fountain, Hoylake Promenade

Massive stone breakwaters have been built below the sea wall. The path above the top of the wall soon meets a wide track. Follow the track. It leads out to a recently-landscaped area known as the North Wirral Coastal Park. Before reaching the lighthouse, leave the track by going to the right, over a small footbridge. The pathway leads you through an area of reeds.

After crossing some old stream channels over footbridges, a narrow road comes in from the right. An extensive turfed and landscaped area lies between the shore and Leasowe lighthouse.

To continue the walk, go inland along a signposted path which leaves the tarmac road about 100 yards beyond the lighthouse, alongside Bankfield House.

The path crosses a field diagonally to the left. It then curves to the left, and runs along the bank of the River Birket to a road. A short walk along to the right leads to the railway station at **Moreton.**

Hoylake

The town gets its name from the 'Hoyle Lake', a large expanse of water which used to lie between sandbanks in Liverpool Bay, directly opposite the present promenade. The lake used to provide a sheltered pool for vessels waiting to enter Liverpool or before going up the estuary of the Dee. In the 1700s the Dee had silted up to such an extent that only very small vessels could get up to Chester – larger vessels anchored in the Hoyle Lake of off Hilbre Island and their cargoes and passengers travelled overland to Chester. The silting of the Dee was accelerated after 1725 by the cutting of a new canalised channel from Chester to Connah's Quay on the Welsh side of the river. In 1700 there was a depth of 15 feet of water in the Hoyle Lake even at low tide, and scores of vessels anchored there. In the early 1800s packet boats travelling between Liverpool and North Wales called at Hoylake to pick up mail and passengers. By 1840 the depth in the Hoyle Lake had dwindled to about 15 feet at high water. Ten years later only half that depth was available and the lake soon disappeared altogether.

A road leading from the railway station to the shore is called 'The King's Gap'. Its name commemorates the passage of the army of King William III on its way to set sail for Ireland in 1690. The army had been encamped for a week at Neston. Some eighty vessels left Hoylake carrying ten thousand men.

Hoylake was an important venue in the horse racing calendar in the last century. Racing began about 1840 and continued until 1876. The meetings were held in May and in August. Both flat races and steeplechases were run.

Hoylake is the home of the Royal Liverpool Golf Club. A course was opened in 1669, initially of nine holes. The club used the prefix 'Royal' when Queen Victoria's son Prince Arthur of Connaught agreed to be made Honorary President in 1871. The course was the venue for the very first British Amateur Championship in 1885. The Open Championship came to Royal Liverpool in 1897 and in many subsequent years.

Hilbre Island

See Note after Walk 4

Meols

Meols is believed to have been the site of a Roman encampment. Many Roman coins and artefacts have been found there over the years. The encampment may have been an outpost of the Roman garrison at Chester. A Roman road seems to have run from Chester through Parkgate in the direction of Meols.

Dove Point, Meols

The ancient village of Meols was gradually engulfed by the sea. It was finally abandoned in the reign of Edward III. The village probably stood out on Dove Point.

Leasowe Lighthouse

Two lighthouses were built at Leasowe in 1763. One of them was soon damaged by the impact of the sea and abandoned. it was replaced by a lighthouse on Bidston Hill in 1771. Both lighthouses were built by Liverpool Corporation. The present house was completed in 1824, to replace the earlier building. The old date stone was fixed into the wall of the new lighthouse. It reads 'W.M.G. 1763'. This commemorates William Gregson, who was mayor of Liverpool in that year. The lighthouse operated until 1908, when buoyed lights in the Mersey approaches made shore lights unnecessary.

Moreton

High tides used to flood the marshes around Wallasey Pool and cover the surrounding land as far as Moreton. The town was taken into the Borough of Wallasey in 1928.

3. WARRINGTON – HOWLEY – PADDINGTON – WOOLSTON – MARTINSCROFT

A walk along part of the Mersey and Irwell Navigation

Distance: 6 miles

Allow: 3 hours

Start: Warrington Central Railway Station (O.S. Ref: SJ 606885)

From Warrington central railway Station, the route to the bank of the Mersey begins by turning left at the station exit and walking up Horsemarket Street and then forward down Bridge Street to its end, at a busy crossroads opposite Wilderspool Causeway. At the end of Bridge Street, do not cross the road yet, but turn sharp left, along Mersey Street.

Walk for about 50 yards, as far as the Royal Insurance building and, using the central reservation, cross the two busy carriageways with great care.

On reaching the safety of the far side, walk to the right and follow the pavement as it curves down to the promenade on the left bank of the Mersey, beyond the furthest road bridge, into the quiet of Wharf Street.

Walk forward along the riverside pavement. Where the line of railings ends, the road bends to the left, past a line of trees. At the end of the tree-line, continue directly forward down a neatly-cobbled pathway.

Passing through a landscaped area on the right-hand side of the modern factory units, one arrives at part of an old wharf, marked with four metal bollards. A short distance further on, a remnant of an old wooden jetty stands at the water's edge.

Some 200 yards ahead, is the chamber of **Howley Lock**. Water cascades through the old timbers of the upper lock gate. (The lock allowed vessels to pass up and down between the Mersey tideway and the Mersey & Irwell Navigation).

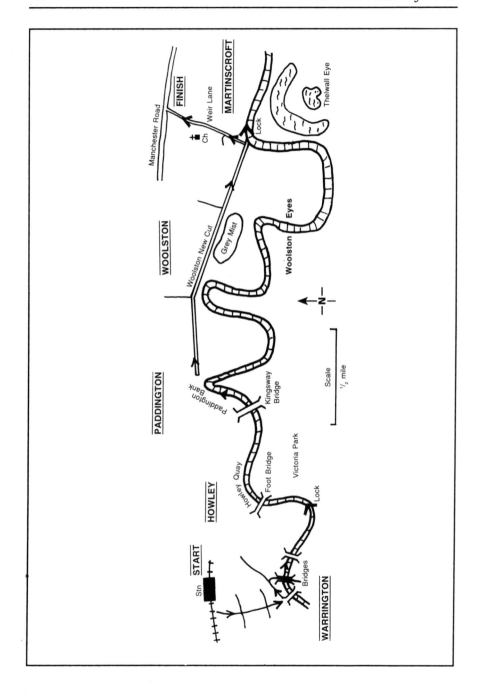

Continuing over the cobbles, the path turns sharp left along the riverside. Over to the right, partly screened-off from view by the trees, the Mersey, having flowed down from Stockport, tumbles over Howley Weir. Visible on the far bank just up-river of the weir, is a small square building. This was once the operator's cabin for a swing bridge which used to span the river.

300 yards of walking, past the houses and between the trees along an earthy pathway, brings you to Howley Footbridge, its elaborate structure hanging high above the river. A few yards beyond the bridge is a picnic area.

A flight of steps leads up to the footbridge. Climb the steps and cross to the other bank. The bridge has a habit of assuming a life of its own as it springs up and down on its suspension cables.

Now go to the left and walk on the right bank along the grassy path. Over on the left there comes into view the Old Quay Tavern, set alongside a couple of disused transit sheds.

The next stretch of river sweeps in a wide arc towards the Kingsway Bridge. Walking alongside the sports field, you reach Manor Lock. This was the entrance from the river to the Runcorn & Latchford Canal. The waterway has been filled in to form the basis of a nature trail leading south-westwards to Latchford and Wilderspool.

After diverting slightly to the right to safely cross the old lock chamber, continue under the small archway and climb the steps on the far side. Cross the busy bridge and resume your walk on the left bank of the river.

Walk upstream along a path behind the allotments. You soon reach a weather-beaten signpost showing the way to Woolston Weir. Continue forward for about 400 yards, between the river and Kingsway North. Go along an avenue of trees and through a fence-gap to the houses at **Paddington Bank**.

Use the pavement and walk in a 200-yard-long curve to a second gated opening in the railings. Go through the gate and continue along the riverside.

Manor Lock (disused), looking towards the old line of the Runcorn and Latchford Canal, now a public footpath.

About 100 yards further on, at the head of a hairpin bend in the river known as Mile's Bite, ignore the obvious right-hand field-path and continue forward. Pass behind the house, to reach the towpath of the old semi-watered line of the **Woolston New Cut**.

The cut, long since belying its name, designed as a navigational channel to bypass three miles of the winding river meanders of the Woolston Eyes, presents, at the time of writing, a scene of awesome desolation. Its entire length is choked with reed beds and an assortment of other vegetation, an area of abandon and neglect but a haven for wildlife.

Less than a mile along the towpath, which in parts still retains its old cobblestones, there is an old planked footbridge at New Cut Lane. Continue your trek, passing a large lake of floodwater which has been rather fancifully called The Grey Mist.

After some 400 yards, continue over Bridge Lane and walk along for about half a mile to the end of the cut at Weir Lane in Martinscroft. The disused keeper's cottage at the cut's exit lock perches up on the far side of the disused old waterway.

Beyond Weir Lane there is an improved signposted pathway along the riverside as far as Swithin Hill Wood in Rixton. On the opposite side of the river stands a high embankment. It was built by the Ship Canal Company to retain the waters of a huge lagoon lying between the Mersey and the ship canal channel at Thelwall.

The day's walk may be completed by turning left and walking up past the church to the Manchester Road. A bus back to Warrington may be boarded at a shelter some 50 yards to the right of the lane end.

Howley

When the Roman legions built a road from their settlement at Wilderspool to Wigan and beyond, they paved a ford on the bed of the Mersey at Latchford to carry the road across the water. In Norman times, a castle used to stand near the parish church at Howley, overlooking and guarding the river crossing. It was around this castle and the church that Howley began to grow.

When the Boteler family, the lords of the manor, moved to Bewsey in 1264, Warrington's focus of growth shifted to the area around the river bridge, leaving Howley on the edge of the town.

The opening of the Runcorn & Latchford Canal in 1804 meant that boats could set off for Runcorn and Liverpool without having to wait for the Mersey tide to come in. Consequently, facilities for barges and their cargoes were built at Howley Quay. Boats which used to call at Warrington's Bank Quay could now berth at Howley, making use of Manor Lock to move up and down between the river and the new canal.

Paddington Bank

When Robert Hatton built a soap works on the river bank in 1820, he called it 'The Paddington Works'. The new name was probably a combination of the names 'Padgate' and 'Warrington'. Hatton had been forced to move out of Warrington and relocate his factory in a district next to Padgate because he had been taken to court for allowing dreadful smells to escape from his Warrington soapery. The new name, first applied to the factory, was later adopted as the name of the district when it came to be built up.

Woolston

This suburb of Warrington was virtually isolated from its larger neighbour for many centuries. There was just an old lane to Warrington and a ferry over the Mersey at Thelwall. The connection to Warrington was improved in the 1750s when a turnpike road to Manchester (now the A75) was built through the village.

The opening of Woolston New Cut in 1821 made the district even busier, linking it to Manchester and Warrington by water as well as by land. Edward Baines painted this word picture of Woolston as he saw it in 1825:

"The communication between Manchester and Liverpool by means of the navigation is incessant and the brick-dust coloured sails of the barges are seen every hour of the day on their passage, flickering in the wind".

4. WEST KIRBY – CALDY – THURSTASTON – HESWALL

This walk travels across countryside on the Wirral shore of the River Dee. It passes through the villages of Caldy and Thurstaston.

Distance: 7 miles

Allow: $4^1/_2$ hours

Start: West Kirby Railway Station (O.S. Ref: SJ 213869)

Begin the walk at West Kirby railway station. Cross the main road and walk up Dee Lane to the riverside promenade.

From the promenade you can look out over the Dee Estuary to where it reaches the sea. To the right are three islands. **Hilbre Island**, the largest, is on the seaward side. Next to it is Little Hilbre. Little Eye is some distance from the other two. When the tide is favourable it is possible to walk across the foreshore to the islands.

Over on the Welsh shore, Point of Air can be seen at the extreme end of a low-lying projection of land. This is the site of a colliery. The mine-workings extend outwards below the sea bed.

Turn left and walk the length of the promenade. The expanse of water which laps against the sea wall is a marina, retained at all states of the tide by a boundary wall about a mile in length.

The Welsh shore visible from the promenade extends from Mostyn, running eastwards up the estuary to Holywell, Flint, and Connah's Quay.

At the end of the promenade, turn left past the boatyard and walk up Sandy Lane. Pass the entrance to Riverside, and take the next turning to the right, up Macdona Drive. This road leads out to Cubbin's Green.

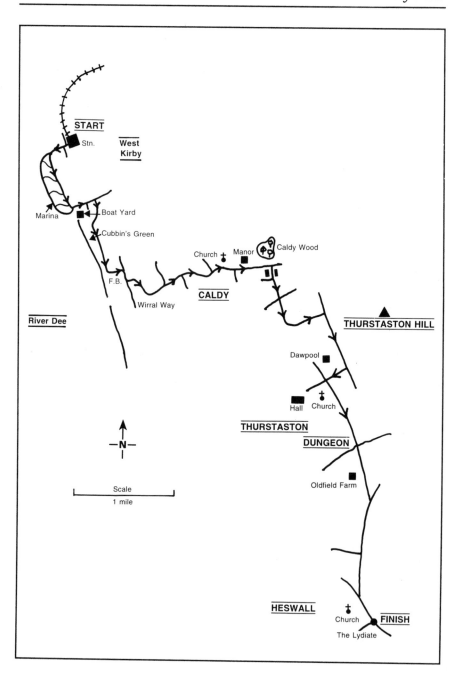

START
Stn.   **West
            Kirby**

Marina   Boat Yard
Cubbin's Green

Church ✝ Manor ■ Caldy Wood

F.B.

CALDY
Wirral Way

River Dee

▲ **THURSTASTON HILL**

Dawpool ■

Hall ■ ✝ Church

THURSTASTON

DUNGEON

Oldfield Farm ■

—N—

Scale
1 mile

HESWALL ✝
            Church ● **FINISH**
            The Lydiate

Walk forward along the grassy river bank. The sea defence along this section of the shore has been recently improved, by means of a barrier of large boulders set down on the beach below.

Where the riverside path ends, bear left, along a gravel path over a footbridge, to reach the **Wirral Way Footpath**. After a few yards, there is a picnic area. The footpath passes between densely-packed trees to reach Shore Road in Caldy.

Turn left and walk up Shore Road to the centre of the village. Continue forward past a crossroads. The road winds uphill between wooded mansions to a T-junction. Turn to the left.

About 100 yards further, you arrive at **Caldy** village green. The grass is raised above the roadway, alongside the church and the old sandstone cottages.

The next part of the journey is to the village of Thurstaston. Begin at the church gate. Turn left, and walk through the village. Many of the cottages bear dated mason's inscriptions. The building on the left with a clock-tower is Caldy Manor. At the time of writing it is in use as a complex of retirement flats. Continue along past Caldy Wood.

Where the road dips, look for a signposted path leading off to the right. Pass between the houses. At the end of this path, continue forward down the road. At the T-junction, walk directly across to enter a track.

Directly ahead is **Thurstaston Hill**, a popular viewing-point. On a lower level is the spire of the church at **Thurstaston**.

The track leads out between fields. Where it begins to curve to the left, go forward over the stile, and then walk along the side of the fence to pass through a bachelor-gate.

Walk to the left, alongside the hedgerow, and reach the A540 road. Turn right, and walk upwards along the road, past Thurstaston Hill. As you climb, the Dee estuary comes into view again. Near the brow of the hill, pass through a deep sandstone cutting. The high ground to the right is known as Thor's Hill.

Beyond a car park and a public house, turn right, down Station Road to Thurstaston village green. Next to the church is **Thurstaston Hall**. The narrow road running right, in the direction of Caldy, leads to the site of the **Dawpool**. Here there used to be a wharf on the river bank. The area has long ago been abandoned by the tides and a house now stands there.

Start the final stage of the walk, to Heswall, by going up the sandy track which runs along the left wall of the churchyard.

The track leads you to a stile. Cross over it and walk along the fenced path over the fields. This way gives a high view of the estuary.

The fields are crossed between hedgerow and fence by means of a succession of stiles. You soon reach the entrance to a wooded creek known as The Dungeon.

The path emerges at **Oldfield Farm** in Heswall. Follow the track past the farm, on to Oldfield Road. Go forward to pass the grounds of the old Cleaver Hospital, which at the time of writing was in the process of demolition.

The walk ends in the oldest part of **Heswall**, known as the 'lower village'. At the end of Oldfield Road, turn right, and walk downhill along Thurstaston Road for about three-quarters of a mile.Pass the entrance of Delavor Road and go down Village Road into old Heswall.

Buses to Birkenhead and Liverpool can be boarded at The Lydiate.

Hilbre Island

The island was the site of a small settlement of Saxon monks of the Benedictine Order. They established a tiny shrine on the island, dedicated to St Hildeburgh, from whom the name 'Hilbre' is derived. Before the dissolution of the monasteries the island was an important place for pilgrims. The settlement was under the supervision of the abbey of St Werburgh at Chester.

The island used to house several families of fishermen. A good deal of smuggling of goods is believed to have gone on in times past – the island is well positioned for the off-loading of contraband goods from vessels heading for Liverpool, or heading up the Dee towards Chester.

A salt refinery was established on Hilbre in 1694. Rock salt was taken overland from the Northwich area to Frodsham and then shipped down the River Weaver to the Mersey. Other rock salt refineries operated at that time at Dungeon Point near Hale and on the edge of the Pool of Liverpool.

Little Hilbre (Middle Eye) was used as a decoy by the anti-aircraft defence forces in the Second World War. Oil fires were set off electrically by cable from Hilbre Island in an attempt to convince enemy pilots that they were entering Liverpool. Other similar decoys were positioned along the Dee shore.

Hilbre is today used as a nature reserve, being situated in one of the most important areas in Britain for visiting bird migrants.

The Wirral Way

This footpath runs between West Kirby and Hooton, a distance of twelve miles. It follows the course of an old railway line, through Caldy, Thurstaston, Parkgate, Neston and Willaston. The line was built as far as Parkgate in 1866 for the transport of coal from Neston colliery to Birkenhead. It was extended to West Kirby in 1886 and became a rail link for commuters. The line was closed to passenger traffic in 1956 and to goods in 1962. The single-track line was removed and replaced by the footpath. The Wirral Way path was opened to the public in 1973.

Caldy

In the Domesday Survey of 1086 the area around Caldy, including Thurstaston and West Kirby, was known as 'Calders'. It was given by Hugh Lupus, Earl of Chester, to Robert de Rodelent. Robert was a military leader who conducted campaigns against the Welsh. He built Rhuddlan Castle and had lands in Wirral and North Wales. He was killed during a Welsh attack on a fortress at Deganwy in 1088.

Caldy stands on the slope of Grange Hill. An old mill at Caldy used to act as a landmark for vessels entering safe anchorage in the Hoyle Lake. No trace of the mill remains, but it is believed to have stood near Caldy Manor House.

The village was once owned by the Norris family of Speke Hall. In 1543 it was sold by Sir William Norris to John Whitemore. The estate remained in the Whitemore family until 1832, when it was sold to Richard Barton, a Manchester merchant. Caldy was in a rather dilapidated condition when Barton bought it. He proceeded to renovate or rebuild every house in the village. The old sandstone cottages bear witness to the success of Barton's improvements.

Richard Barton built Caldy Manor House. In 1882 part of this building was converted into a chapel and the clock tower was added. It served as a place of worship until the opening of the church in 1907. The church contains within its structure the old school house of 1868. The sandstone cross on the green by the church is in memory of Alfred Barton, who died in 1839. The Caldy estate was bought in 1906 by the Caldy Manor Estates Company. The Manor House is at present in use as a complex of retirement homes.

Thurstaston Hill

This sandstone outcrop is split into two parts by the West Kirby-Chester road. The larger inland part of the hill links up with Thurstaston Common. The highest point is 300 feet above sea level. In 1883, 45 acres of the land were given jointly to Birkenhead Corporation and the Overseers of the Poor of the parish of Thurstaston. A further 98 acres were later given to the National Trust under the corporation's management.

A massive sandstone boulder on the hill was given the name 'Thor's Stone'. It has over the years been suggested that the stone was a place of worship for Norse settlers. No firm evidence of such use has ever been found. However, Thurstaston could well have been settled by incoming Norsemen. Its name may be derived from 'Thurstan's tun', meaning 'Thurstan's farm', but again this is speculation.

Thurstaston Church

There have been two previous churches on the site of the present building. The earliest record of a church at Thurstaston is 1125. Until 1724 a church stood in the grounds of the adjacent Hall before being demolished in 1820. In 1824 a plain low building with a small tower was built. It was pulled down in the 1880s and replaced by the present building. Today's church was built as a memorial to Joseph Hegan of nearly Dawpool by his two daughters. It opened in 1886.

Dawpool

The name 'Dawpool' was at one time used to fix the position of a small group of dwellings on the river bank. The Dawpool was a small harbour for vessels. Together with the ports at Parkgate and Neston, Dawpool came into use by vessels that were unable to reach Chester owing to the progressive silting of the Dee's navigation channel. A shipping manual of 1693 included the following advice: *"If you would sail up to Dort-Pool and Nesson you must have a care of the out Scar-Rocks....You may Anchor at Dort-Pool in three Fathom water"*.

Dean Jonathan Swift, the satirical writer, author of 'Gulliver's Travels', landed at Dawpool from Dublin in 1707 and sailed from there to Ireland in 1709.

Dawpool House was built in 1884 for Thomas Henry Ismay, the founder of the Oceanic Steamship Company (the 'White Star Line'). Born in Maryport, Cumbria in 1837, Ismay was the son of a shipbuilder. His widow gave the east window of Liverpool Anglican Cathedral in memory of her husband.

Oldfield Farm

The farm was originally used as a dwelling called Oldfield Hall. It was the hall of the manor of Oldfield, which used to exist separately from Heswall. In Elizabethan times the house was the home of a Cheshire courtier called Sir Rowland Stanley. At the age of 86 he married his third wife and in 1604 moved with her from Hooton to live at Oldfield Hall. After ten years of marriage he died in 1614, aged 96, and was buried in Eastham Church.

Heswall

The present town of Heswall developed this century from the separate villages of Oldfield, Gayton, and the old village of Heswall. In 1875, the church at Heswall was struck by lightning during an evening service. The organist and a boy operating the organ bellows were killed and the main body of the building was destroyed by the resulting fire. Only the tower of the old building now remains, part of which dates back to the fourteenth century.

Thurstaston Hall

The hall stands next to the church. The original hall and church are believed to have stood together, surrounded by fortifications as protection against attack from the Welsh armies. The present hall was built in the late 1600s by the Whitemore family, who had been lords of the manor of Thurstaston since the fourteenth century.

5. ACTON BRIDGE – CROWTON – PICKERING'S CUT – DUTTON LOCKS – ACTON BRIDGE

This circular walk passes through the Cheshire countryside along the Weaver Valley.

Distance: 8 miles

Allow: $3^1/_2$ hours

Start: Acton Bridge Railway Station (O.S. Ref: SJ 598743)

On leaving the railway station at **Acton Bridge,** pass the Hazel Pear Inn. Turn left on to a signposted footpath which leads off the road, just beyond the inn's car park. Follow this path along a boundary fence. Cross the stile into a field.

Go across the centre of the field to cross the next stile. A series of fields is then crossed. Several of the stiles have been waymarked in yellow. The last stile leads out to a track. On the far side of this stile, be careful to step over a narrow gully.

Bear left along the track, over the railway bridge. Follow the track to the right, alongside the railway line. The long high ridge of land visible on the left leads out to Frodsham. Continue over the stiles to reach a lane by a bridge at Lower Green Farm.

At the bridge, ignore the yellow arrow pointing ahead. Instead, turn left to walk down the lane which leads away from the bridge.

After about 100 yards, there is a junction. Continue forward along the lane and enter a narrow track between hedges. This track leads downhill over a muddy old cobbled pavement to reach the bank of Acton Brook.

Cross the brook and pass through the gateway. Just beyond the gate, turn to the immediate right, to follow the field-path along the edge of

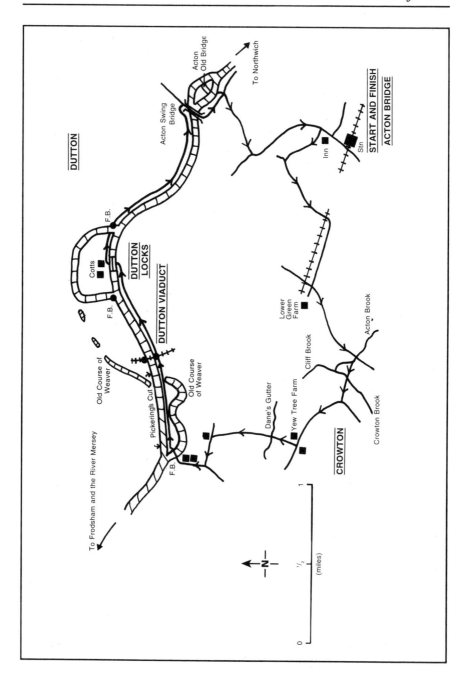

the brook. Cross over the long footbridge into the next field.

A few yards to the right of this footbridge is the junction of three brooks. Acton brook comes the way you have travelled. Crowton Brook flows under the footbridge. The two combine to form Cliff Brook, which flows away northwards to the River Weaver.

Walk away from the footbridge exit, over the hilly field, past an isolated tree in its centre. Climb over the stile by the gate, on to a track.

Turn left and walk for some 30 yards only, to reach a T-junction in Crowton. At the junction walk to the right, up the tarmac road.

After about 300 yards, look for a signposted track leading away to the right, just beyond Yew Tree Farm. Follow this track to the left of the buildings. Climb over the gate into the field. Now walk to the left and follow the hedgerow of the field as it swings to the right. Keeping the hedge to your left, walk down the field edge into a gully called Dane's Gutter. As you do so, the arches of the Dutton Viaduct are in view ahead.

Cross the gutter over a bank, and then continue upwards to a stile set in the corner of the field. Go over the stile and walk forward alongside the hedge to cross another stile, on to a tarmac lane by some cottages.

Walk to the left along the lane to a T-junction. At the junction, turn right, and walk down past some more cottages to a footbridge on the crown of the bend.

This bridge crosses an old part of the River Weaver which was left behind when Pickering's Cut was made. Cross the bridge and walk down the path through an avenue of trees to reach the bank of the Weaver Navigation.

This is where **Pickering's Lock** used to be. The position of the lock gates can be seen in the stone walls on the opposite bank. A short distance to the left, the old Weaver flows into the artificial navigation.

The next part of the journey follows the bank of the navigation along Pickering's Cut for about a mile to Dutton Locks.

The sandstone **Dutton Viaduct** carries the Liverpool-Crewe railway over the navigation. It was built a few years after the Sankey Viaduct, which is passed on Walk No. 15.

To the right, in front of the viaduct, a remnant of the old river is in service for fishing. It ends in front of the railway embankment.

Cross the stile beneath the viaduct and walk along the bank in the direction of Dutton Locks. Vessels at present are allowed to pass only through a single archway. The other one has been barricade off owing to an insufficient depth of water being available to the larger vessels.

Beyond the viaduct, a footbridge on the opposite bank, built upon long straddling arches, crosses the junction between the navigation and another section of the old river. A single small chalet stands up against the trees to the right. The riverbank pathway leads over a stile to reach **Dutton Locks**. A neatly-grassed area with seating is available here.

Resume the walk by crossing over the lock gates to reach the opposite side of the locks. Exercise every care and attention. Pass in front of the lock keepers' cottages and continue along the path on the bank, towards the **Acton Swing Bridge**. Cross the footbridge over a junction with the old river and walk down the tarmac lane along the curving bank of the wide navigation.

When you reach the swing bridge, go up, cross the road, and then walk over the bridge using the footwalk on its far side. A little way upstream from the swing bridge stands the old Acton stone bridge. It now spans a short section of the old Weaver to reach an island between the two waterways.

Walk along the main road for about 200 yards to reach the junction with Acton Lane. Carefully cross over. Walk up Acton Lane. A footpath begins along the wide grass verge on the left side of this road.

The road climbs steeply out of the Weaver Valley. It levels out at Strawberry Lane and leads you forward to a T-junction. The way is now to the left, along Hill Top Road.

A cottage on the right, on the corner of Old Lane, is dated 1702. The road passes the Maypole Inn and the village post office before going down past the Hazel Pear Inn to the railway station.

Acton Bridge

The village has grown very little over the years. The census returns for 1881 and 1971 give population figures of 227 and 276. In 1967 the name of the parish was officially changed from Acton to Acton Bridge, in order to distinguish it from another Cheshire village called Acton, situated about a mile north-east of Nantwich.

Pickering's Lock and Cut

Pickering's Boat was the old tidal limit of the Weaver before the first improvement work of the 1730's. It was the site of a lock on the original navigation. The final improvements to the lock were completed in 1850. In the twenty-year period after 1875 a large programme of improvement work was put into effect on the navigation. It was in this period that the channel was deepened and the lock removed. The stone house on the canal bank used to belong to the manager of the navigation.

Dutton Viaduct

The viaduct was built as part of the Grand Junction Railway, opened in 1837 to link Birmingham with Liverpool and Manchester via Warrington. It was designed by Robert Stephenson. The viaduct has twenty arches, each of which has a span of sixty feet. It is some sixty feet high.

Dutton Locks

These locks were built in 1876 during a series of improvements to the navigation. The two locks were designed to accommodate the newly-introduced steam packets, each of which towed a line of three narrow boats. The larger lock is 229ft long and $42^{1}/_{2}$ft wide. The smaller has a length of 220ft and a width of 24ft. There is a depth of 15ft of water over the lock sills. The rise in level is 8ft.

Acton Swing Bridge

The bridge carries the A49 Warrington-Northwich road. A short distance upstream are the foundations of an earlier swing bridge. The present structure has some $3/5$ths of its weight supported by buoyancy tanks. The swing mechanism is hydraulically operated. The bridge was built in 1932.

6. OLD ROAN – LEEDS & LIVERPOOL CANAL – AINTREE RACE COURSE – MELLING – NETHERTON – MAGHULL

A canal walk on the edge of the metropolis which passes the race course and includes a visit to the village of Melling

Distance: 6 miles

Allow: 3 hours

Start: Old Roan (O.S. Ref: SJ 370993)

From the Liverpool side of the Old Roan Inn, cross at the traffic lights and enter a path which runs from the right-hand foot of the high humped main road bridge. The path leads you behind the right side of the roadway. After a few yards you reach the towing path of the Leeds & Liverpool Canal.

Turn left and walk along the towing path in the direction of Aintree, passing beneath the road bridge. After about 400 yards, the race course grandstands can be seen, beyond the boundary wall.

The next bridge carries the Melling road over the canal. Just beyond this bridge, the steeplechase course comes into view. On the left is the suburb of Aintree, with neat and tidy semi-detached properties.

The view from the canal gradually opens out. Along this section there are good views over the race course. This corner of the course is the famous "Canal Turn". The riders have to approach the canal, clear the obstacle, and after only a few yards, swing their horses to the left, to make their way parallel to the canal. In the early years of the **Grand National**, the canal was not fenced off as it is today. Many a horse ignored the turn and carried its despairing jockey into the chilly water.

Continuing the walk, the district known as Fazakerley lies to the right of the canal. The tall red-brick clock tower is at the Cottage Homes. These

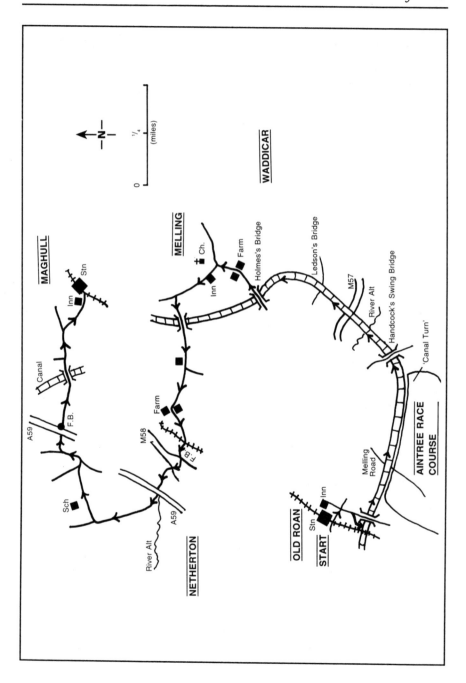

were built for children in the care of the West Derby Union under the old Poor Law system.

Pass beneath a footbridge to reach Handcock's Swing Bridge. A grassed area is available on the opposite bank. Continue the walk by crossing the roadway. The towing path continues beyond the bridge.

The next part of the journey is to the village of **Melling**. The tower of Melling church can be seen in the distance to the left. Ahead, the M57 motorway runs across the line of the canal. Beyond the motorway, there are several buildings. These are in the hamlet called Waddicar. The tall tower blocks on the right are in Kirkby.

The canal passes over the River Alt along a short aqueduct. It then travels beneath the motorway and then under Waddicar Lane at Ledson's Bridge. Two small factories are passed, and then Melling comes into view. The village can be seen up on a hill to the right.

The canal curves to the left and the path comes to Holmes's Swing Bridge. Leave the canal path by crossing the bridge to the lane on the opposite bank. Walk up the lane between the buildings of New House Farm. Beyond the farm, the lane winds gently upwards to a road junction. At the junction, take the left fork. After a short walk along Rock Lane, you arrive at the Bootle Arms Inn and the parish church of St. Thomas.

Begin the journey from Melling to Maghull by continuing down the hillside along Rock Lane. After about 200 yards a road junction is reached. Turn left, along Brewery Lane. Walk up and over the canal via a narrow humped bridge. (It is safer to cross the bridge on the left side of the roadway to avoid any difficulties with oncoming vehicles.)

The road curves to the left by a small row of houses. At the bend, continue directly forward along a narrow tarmac lane. Any signs reading "Private Road" are for the benefit of drivers. The lane is a public path for travellers on foot.

The lane bears left to pass between the buildings of Wood Hall Farm. Beyond the farm, a track runs between unfenced fields to the embankment of the Liverpool-Ormskirk railway.

Pass under the railway through an arched opening. The pathway winds to the left. Use the footbridge to cross the carriageway of the M58 motorway.

The path is retained between lines of fencing. It leads to a short subway beneath the second carriageway. Follow the path behind the houses alongside Dover's Brook to emerge at the busy A59 road. The pathway continues on the opposite side of the dual-carriageway.

Make **no** attempt to cross the road at this point. Instead, turn right, and make your way along the road to cross carefully using the central reservation.

Having crossed the road, walk back to the left. A signpost shows where the pathway continues. Walk along the bank of the Alt for a few yards, before going up to a track on an embankment. This embankment was built to carry the Aintree-Southport railway over the river and onwards to Maghull. From this vantage point, the steeple of Sefton church can be seen to the left. Houses in Maghull are on the right.

After walking along the track for about half a mile, look for a path running off to the right. It begins by a pylon, and runs along the boundary fence of a school playing field. The path goes down a short flight of steps and over a footbridge. Follow the path between the brook and the fence to emerge at Ormonde Drive.

Bear right for a few yards to the main road. Cross over. Turn left, and after some 100 yards, go to the right, along Hall Lane. Cross the dual-carriageway via the footbridge. Walk along the second portion of Hall Lane. After about 300 yards, rejoin the canal at a swing bridge.

Maghull railway station can be reached by crossing the bridge and walking directly forward. The road bends to the right by a church. It leads to the Great Mogul Inn, the shops, and the station.

The Grand National

In 1827 William Lynn, the owner of the Waterloo Hotel in Liverpool, opened a flat course at Aintree. In 1836 Lynn introduced an event called the Grand Liverpool Steeplechase. This race was run annually on a course at Maghull until 1839, when the race was brought to Aintree. In 1847 a journalist invented the name 'Grand National' and this name was kept.

Melling

The village is built on a sandstone hill. It used to be surrounded by the marshland around the River Alt. In the late 6th century Melling was occupied by Anglian settlers. These people came across the Pennines from Yorkshire and Durham. (Similar settlements of this period have the suffix 'ing' in their names, like Billinge. There is another Melling on the banks of the River Lune, to the north of Lancaster.

At the time of the Domesday Survey, Melling was in the possession of Godiva, the widow of Leofric, Earl of Mercia. A huge forest stretched from nearby Waddicar ('Wood Acre') to Wood End in Maghull.

Melling has always been an agricultural area. However, at the turn of the century a pottery and gun-cotton works were in operation. The church on the hilltop was built in 1835.

7. MAGHULL – LEEDS & LIVERPOOL CANAL – CHESHIRE LINES PATH – LYDIATE – LEEDS & LIVERPOOL CANAL – MAGHULL

This circular walk includes a section along a recently improved public footpath situated between the Leeds & Liverpool Canal and the River Alt

Distance: 8 miles

Allow: $3^1/_2$ hours

Start: Maghull Railway Station (O.S. Ref: SD 384015)

From the railway station at Maghull, make your way to the towing-path of the Leeds & Liverpool Canal. Turn right at the station exit. Pass the Great Mogul Inn and the shops, and walk along to St George's church.

Follow the road as it curves leftwards. At the next right-hand bend, leave the road a go forward over the narrow swing-bridge. Turn right, on to the towing-path. Several cottages on the opposite bank have gardens laid out on the canal-side behind them.

After about a mile, leave the canal path to rejoin it later in Lydiate. The fields next to the canal help to retain the rural character of this part of Maghull, despite the steady growth of the town in recent years.

Pass under road bridge No. 12A, and continue forward to go beneath an old bridge. This has a more modern metalled footpath alongside it.

About 200 yards further, turn left at a swing-bridge to leave the canal path and walk down Shop Lane. On reaching a T-junction, cross the road. Turn right and walk to the left, away from the roundabout at the second opening, and enter the narrow portion of Green Lane.

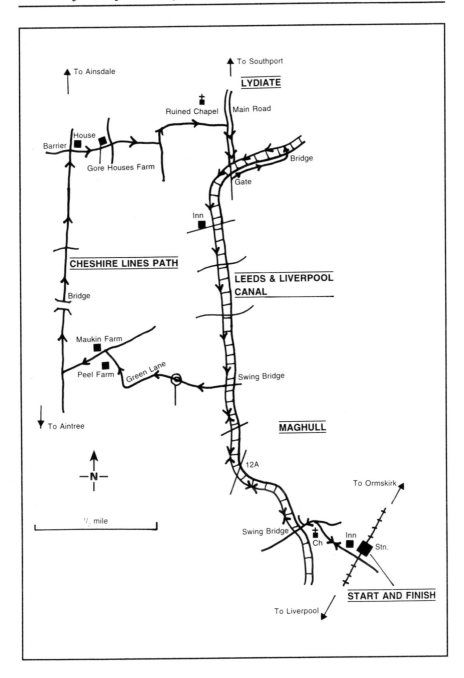

To Ainsdale

To Southport

LYDIATE

Ruined Chapel

Main Road

Barrier

House

Gore Houses Farm

Bridge

Gate

Inn

CHESHIRE LINES PATH

LEEDS & LIVERPOOL CANAL

Bridge

Maukin Farm

Peel Farm

Green Lane

Swing Bridge

To Aintree

—N—

¹/₂ mile

MAGHULL

12A

To Ormskirk

Swing Bridge

Ch

Inn

Stn.

START AND FINISH

To Liverpool

The hedgerow in front of the right-hand pavement of this lane has been kept in position, in an attempt to screen the two rows of houses from each other. When this was written, house-building was rapidly eating up the farmland in this locality.

Follow Green Lane as it curves to the right. Look for the church spire in Sefton village, about a mile away to the left.

The country lane passes the entrance to Peel Farm. At the next bend in the land, alongside Maukin Farm, enter a gravelled lane. It runs along the side of the farm.

After a few hundred yards, there is a wide public path. Turn right and walk along the path towards Lydiate. This path runs from Maghull to Formby, following the direction of a railway line. The line used to run from Aintree to Southport.

Following representations to West Lancashire council by rambling associations and others, the path was improved and opened as a public footpath in 1988. It is at present known as the **Cheshire Lines Path**, after the railway company. It would seem likely that it will be renamed. A separate bridleway has been cut through alongside the footpath.

The woodland on the left horizon surrounds the old halls at Crosby and Ince Blundell. Nearer on the left, the Alt flows between floodbanks out to the sea near Altcar.

Pass beneath a metal-sided bridge. Just beyond this bridge, a path on the left leads up to some seats where the surrounding countryside can be viewed from a higher position.

Continue along the main pathway, beyond a crossing of paths. ignore any paths leading off to the right at this stage of the walk. At the next metal gateway and barrier, pass through and turn to the immediate right, to leave the footpath. Walk along the road. Pass Gore Houses Farm and reach Altcar Lane at a T-junction.

Cross over and enter Punnells Lane, slightly to the left of the junction. You are now walking to rejoin the canal in Lydiate. At the next junction, go to the left, past a short row of houses. On the left of this road are the remains of **St Katherine's Chapel**. It was built as a private chapel, and used by the lords of the manor of Lydiate.

Continue forward along Station Road to reach the main Southport road. At this road, turn right. The canal bridge is about 400 yards along. A path leads away from the left side of the humped bridge, through a small gate.

Go down the steps and walk to the right, along the canal-side. The path soon leads to a small bridge. Cross over to reach the towing-path on the opposite bank, via a flight of steps leading down to the left.

Walk back to Maghull. The direction is such that the canal is on your left side. The return distance along the canal path is about three miles.

You soon pass Lydiate Boat Club's house and marina, near bridge No. 17. Pass the swing-bridge by the Running Horses Inn. A second swing-bridge is passed, a road bridge and then the Green Lane swing-bridge.

Walk beyond Green Lane, and at the next swing-bridge, leave the towing-path. Cross over and go forward along the road. It curves to the right and leads back to the railway station.

Maghull

The first settlements in Maghull were made on land which rises from the low-lying area alongside the River Alt. The western side of the town, between the canal and the Alt, is today still chiefly farmland. It has been reclaimed by drainage of the marshes.

The opening of the canal in 1774 boosted the production of agricultural and dairy produce. These were shipped to Liverpool to feed its rapidly growing population. The coming of the railway to the town in 1850 stimulated both trade and growth. Large villas were built for wealthy Liverpool merchants.

During the Second World War the canal was chosen as a line of defence in the event of the enemy landing on the coast near Formby, a few miles to the west. Concrete blockhouses were built alongside the canal. Several of them remain there today.

Maghull has expanded steadily since 1945. It continues to grow. The population more than doubled between 1951 and 1971 to a figure of 22,000.

In the grounds of St Andrew's Church in Damfield Lane is the Maghull Chapel. It is the oldest religious building on Merseyside, dating from about 1300.

Cheshire Lines Path

The footpath follows the course of a railway line which used to run between Aintree and Southport (Lord Street). The line opened in 1884. It was closed in 1952 and the track was removed. It is hoped to link this footpath at Aintree to a similar path, built upon an old loop line. This second line used to run across the city to Aintree from Halewood, passing through Gateacre, Knotty Ash, West Derby and Walton.

St Katherine's Chapel

This ruined building is sometimes referred to as 'Lydiate Abbey'. It was a chapel, built about 1500, for the use of the lords of the old manor of Lydiate. It is likely that the villagers used to attend services there too.

After the Reformation the building was closed and began to tumble down. Masses were held in secret in nearby Lydiate Hall. The chapel was at last replaced in 1854 by the church of St Mary, built at the expense of Thomas Weld Blundell.

8. LYDIATE – HALL LANE – ALTCAR LANE – DOWNHOLLAND – LEEDS & LIVERPOOL CANAL – LYDIATE

The walk passes firstly across the fields and lanes of Lydiate and Downholland, before returning along the towing-path of the Leeds & Liverpool Canal.

Distance: 7 miles

Allow: 3 hours

Start: Weld Blundell Hotel (O.S. Ref: SD 368041)

From the bus stop at **Lydiate** village green, opposite the Weld Blundell Hotel, carefully cross the road to the hotel and walk forward in the direction of Southport.

About 200 yards along, there is a humped bridge which crosses the Leeds & Liverpool Canal. Enter the path leading away from the right-hand parapet of the bridge. It is signposted 'Pygon's Hill Lane'. This path runs along the canal bank. The old towing-path is on the opposite bank.

Follow the path between the trees to a small canal bridge. Cross the bridge and go forward beyond it along a worn path. The high ground of Clieves Hills can be seen on the right, with the church at Ormskirk standing above. Aughton village and its church spire are visible closer on lower ground on the right. The tower of **St Mary's Church** is in view to the left.

Cross a stile and walk along the field-edge, behind Hill Top Farm. Cross the horse track to the opposite stile. Beyond the track, the path follows the paling fence. Go over the horse-track again, using the stiles.

Pass through a small gate on the right. Bear leftwards and upwards along the fence. At the fence-corner, go to the right, following the

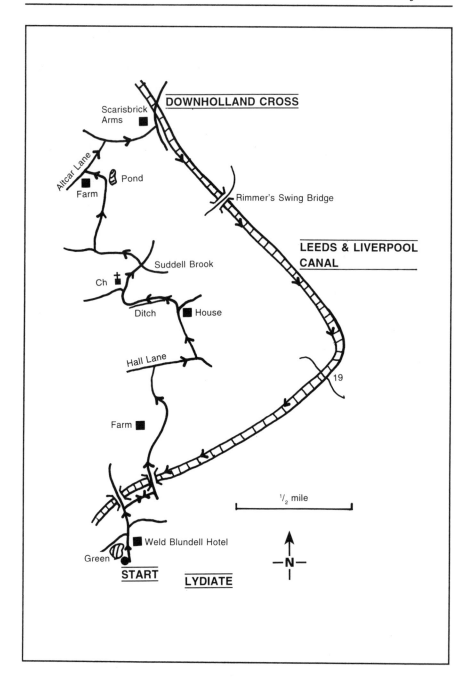

DOWNHOLLAND CROSS

Scarisbrick Arms

Altcar Lane

Pond

Farm

Rimmer's Swing Bridge

LEEDS & LIVERPOOL CANAL

Suddell Brook

Ch

Ditch

House

Hall Lane

19

Farm

½ mile

Weld Blundell Hotel

Green

START

LYDIATE

—N—

white-topped posts, along the right edge of the field to arrive opposite the houses in Hall Lane. Turn right at the lane, pass the school, and take the left turning at the junction.

Where the lane bends sharply to the right at the house, go directly forward along the signposted footpath. It runs along the right side of the hedgerow.

The path curves to the left to reach a long ditch. Cross over to the right side of the ditch and follow the path in the direction of the left-hand boundary of the farm-buildings, to reach the Southport road. At the road, turn right. Cross over to **St Thomas's Parish Church**, and continue forward along Mairscough Lane.

Pass the entrance of Church Farm. About 100 yards further on, the road crosses Suddell Brook. This is the Merseyside boundary, and one enters **Downholland**.

Pause at the first ditch on the left past the bridge. Turn left and walk away from the road along the field-edge to the left side of the ditch. Reach the bank of the brook.

Bear right and walk along the brookside for about fifty yards only. Turn right and walk across the field, aiming for a point between the end farm-building and the circle of trees.

When approaching the farm, walk along the right edge of a ditch, along a cart track. Pass between the back of the farm and the pond, finally bearing left to pass between the buildings, along a wide track, and arrive at Altcar Lane. Here, turn right, and walk in the direction of Ormskirk. The road bends to the right, past the entrance of Blackamoor Lane, to reach the Scarisbrick Arms at Downholland Cross.

Reach the towing-path of the Leeds & Liverpool Canal by using the path and steps situated directly across the T-junction, between the two signposts labelled 'Delf Lane' and 'Mairscough Lane'.

Canal-side seats are available to the left, on the towing-path by the road bridge. The towing-path of the canal can now be followed for some three miles, back to the Weld Blundell.

The direction along the path is to the right, away from the road bridge. About a mile along the path, you pass Rimmer's Swing Bridge. Some three-quarters of a mile further, one walks beneath Lydiate Hall Bridge (No. 19).

The next bridge is narrow. Leave the canal here, and climb up to the bridge, using the steps on its far side. Cross the bridge to the path on the opposite bank. Turn right, go along this path and walk back to the Southport road. By turning left at the road, within a few minutes you reach the Weld Blundell.

Lydiate

The manor of Lydiate was for many years in the possession of the Blundell and the Weld Blundell families. The remains of the manor house, Lydiate Hall, stand at the top of Hall Lane, alongside the Southport Road. The hall was built in 1485. The main part of the building was pulled down in 1780.

St Mary's Church, Lydiate

The church was opened in 1854. It is built of stone quarried at Up Holland. Most of the building costs were borne by Thomas Weld Blundell. In 1871 an ancient stone wayside cross was found by a farm worker in a field by the Southport road, between Lydiate and Downholland. The cross was put up in the cemetery. Five similar crosses had previously been discovered within a mile of Lydiate.

St Thomas's Church, Lydiate

Built in 1839, it became the parish church in 1871, when Lydiate was separated from the parish of Halsall.

Downholland

The village is listed in the Domesday Survey. Until 1290, it was known as 'Holland'. It may have been given its present name in order to distinguish it from Up Holland, which lies further east, towards Wigan.

9. DOWNHOLLAND – LEEDS & LIVERPOOL CANAL – HASKAYNE – HALSALL – LEEDS & LIVERPOOL CANAL – DOWNHOLLAND

This walk explores the paths, lanes and canal in an area to the north of that visited in Walk 8.

Distance: $7^1/_2$ miles

Allow: 3 hours

Start: Scarisbrick Arms Hotel, Downholland (O.S. Ref: SD 365068)

Start the walk at the Scarisbrick Arms Hotel in **Downholland**. The walk begins with a journey to Haskayne along the canal towing path. A narrow path runs down to the canal side. It starts on the approach to the bridge between two signposts marked "Delf Lane" and "Mairscough Lane".

Walk under the road bridge numbered 20A, along the towing path towards Haskayne. On the left side can be seen a scattering of cottages and farms between the canal and the Altcar district. The parish of Aughton lies beyond the road on the higher ground on the right hand side.

After about a quarter of a mile, there is a swing bridge. Just to the left are the old buildings of Downholland Hall. Continue towards Haskayne. At the edge of the village, some of the cottages on the left have thatched roofs. An electricity station is passed as the village is approached.

The path curves to reach a road bridge numbered 21A. Walk to the left, up the flight of steps to the road. The bridge makes a good viewing point over the canal. From the bridge, walk to the left, down the slope to the King's Arms Inn.

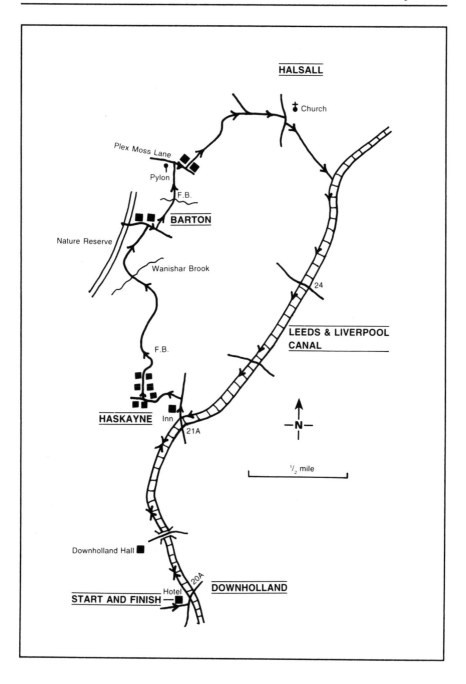

HALSALL

✝ Church

Plex Moss Lane

Pylon

F.B.

BARTON

Nature Reserve

Wanishar Brook

24

F.B.

LEEDS & LIVERPOOL
CANAL

HASKAYNE   Inn

21A

—N—

¹/₂ mile

Downholland Hall ■

20A

START AND FINISH —   Hotel ■   DOWNHOLLAND

Just beyond the inn, turn left along School Lane into the centre of Haskayne. An old thatched cottage is reached on the crown of the bend. Notice the external stairway leading to an upper room.

Continue along School Lane on the right side of the road, past the post office on the opposite side. Turn right, between the houses, along Riding Lane. After about fifty yards, turn right, into Jackson Close. Continue to the end of this cul-de-sac.

Look for a footpath leading off to the left, into a field. This path leads to Barton. Follow the field path along the side of the end house. Beyond the house, do **not** cross the footbridge. Instead, walk along the field edge which runs forward to the left side of the ditch. The path leads out to the curve of a track. Go forward along the left fork, towards the pylon.

Cross a stream called Wanishar Brook and reach the boundary of an old railway cutting. This area is known as the **Haskayne Cutting Nature Reserve**. Legal access to the reserve is achieved only with a permit from the Lancashire Trust for Nature Conservation.

The public footpath is to the right. It runs between the edge of the field and the boundary fence. Continue along the edge of a second field, to arrive at a road in the hamlet of Barton.

Walk to the right, along the road, past a pair of houses dated '1908'. A few yards along on the left is a footpath signposted 'Plex Moss Lane'. Follow this path in a straight line, in the direction of the central house of the five buildings in view ahead. Look out for a ditch running directly across your path. When you reach the ditch, cross the footbridge. Having crossed the ditch, go forward towards the pylon. Walk between the pylon and the end house, up a short slope, to arrive at **Plex Moss Lane**.

Across the lane, the village of Halsall and its church steeple are in view. Go down to the right. Enter a path on the left, which runs between the end house and the house No. 1. This path leads to Halsall.

Go forward down the path alongside the hedge for some 300 yards to reach a track. Keep on in the same direction along the track. The track then brings you to Carr Moss Lane in Halsall.

We now return to the canal. At the road, turn right and walk along to a T-junction. At the junction, cross the road. Enter a gravelled track slightly to the right. This way leads between the fields to the canal. Ahead on the horizon are the Clieves Hills in Aughton.

At the towing path, turn right. Return to the Scarisbrick Arms, passing Barton and Haskayne on the way.

The first bridge passed is numbered 24. The bridge at the journey's end at Downholland is 20A. Buses to Liverpool stop at the small wooden shelter about fifty yards from the hotel.

Downholland

See Note after Walk 8.

Haskayne Nature Reserve

The reserve has been established by the Lancashire Trust for Nature Conservation in an abandoned railway cutting. The railway was a branch line which used to run from Hillhouse Junction, north of Altcar, to Southport Central station. Stations were situated at Barton, Plex Moss Lane, Halsall, and New Cut Lane. The line was opened in 1887. It was closed to passenger traffic in 1938 and goods traffic ceased in 1952.

Plex Moss Lane

A railway halt at Plex Moss Lane was situated on the south side of the bridge. The site is passed on the walk. The station operated from 1906 until the closure of the line in 1938.

Halsall

The village of Halsall stands upon a sandstone outcrop. The land to the west of Halsall used to be a large area of peat moss and marshland. Three lakes or 'meres' used to exist within Halsall Moss. They were known as 'Black Otter', 'White Otter', and 'Gettern'. The rich agricultural land through which the canal runs was reclaimed from the Moss in the last century by the River Alt Drainage Scheme. Many long drainage channels carry excess water away from the low-lying land into the Alt. In the early 1800s a type of inflammable wood used to be dug out of the Moss. This was split into long laths and used by the local population instead of candles.

The church at Halsall was once the place of worship for people living in a wide area around the village. The parish of Halsall used to cover some nine miles from east to west. It included Maghull, Lydiate, Downholland and Melling within its boundaries. The bells of Halsall church used to be rung as darkness fell, to guide travellers home across the moss. The present church of St Cuthbert received its latest rebuilding and alteration work in 1886. Built into the church is a portion dating from the 16th century which used to be a school. The lower part of the steeple used to be a tower, built around 1430. The spire was added later, before being rebuilt in 1852.

Construction of the Leeds & Liverpool Canal began at Halsall. Its first sod was ceremonially cut there in 1770.

10. BURSCOUGH JUNCTION – RING O'BELLS – HOSCAR – PRESCOTT BRIDGE – GLOVER'S BRIDGE – BURSCOUGH JUNCTION

This journey includes walks along the Rufford branch and the main line of the Leeds & Liverpool Canal.

Distance: 8 miles

Allow: $3^1/_2$ hours

Start: Burscough Junction Station (O.S. Ref: SD 445115)

From the Junction Hotel in **Burscough** cross to the pavement and go over the narrow humped bridge which spans the railway line. After 200 yards or so, turn left along Square Lane. This road leads to the Leeds & Liverpool Canal.

Pass the entrance of an army depot. On the left at the bottom of the hill is Wheat Lane. This lane leads to Glover's Swing Bridge which carries the highway over the canal. Cross the bridge to reach the towing-path. Turn right, and walk away from Burscough in the direction of Wigan. After about 100 yards the canal crosses Eller Brook, which flows into the River Douglas near Rufford.

The hills to the left stand above Parbold. Ahead, beyond Skelmersdale is **Ashurst Hill** with its **beacon**. Pass under the road bridge at the Ring o'Bells and continue to Moss Bridge (No. 35).

Leave the canal path by climbing the flight of steps alongside this bridge. Turn left and walk towards the row of cottages. At the cross-roads, turn right along Hollowford Lane.

The next section of the walk takes you through the hamlet of **Hoscar**, and across Hoscar Moss to reach the Rufford Branch of the canal.

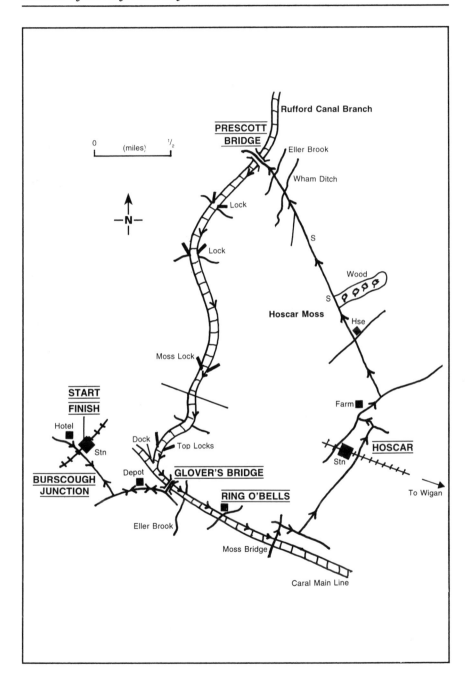

At the last house along the road, turn left along Frog Lane. This narrow lane leads to a level crossing on the Southport-Wigan railway line. Hoscar station is on the left.

Cross the line with care and walk forward to a junction. Turn left and reach a T-junction at the end of Dean's Lane. Turn right and walk along the Hoscar Moss Road past Sandyways Farm. After about 200 yards, turn left along Wood Lane. This is your direction for about two miles.

Walking across the flat reclaimed land of Hoscar Moss you can see Burscough, away to the left. The scattered dwellings in Bispham are to the right of the lane.

Pass the single house at the corner of Bleak Lane and continue forward along a rough track. At the edge of a wood pass over a stile. Maintain your direction along the field-edge, over a second stile, to reach a tarmac lane. Walk ahead towards the canal. Look for the spire of Rufford church at the edge of the line of trees on the horizon, a little to the right.

The lane passes over a drainage channel known as Wham Ditch. At the next bridge, re-cross Eller Brook. The Rufford canal branch is some 300 yards further along the lane, at Prescott Bridge.

Go down a short path to the left of the bridge on to the towing-path. The next part of the walk follows the canal path to the junction with the main canal line near Burscough. A few hundred yards along, climb upwards to pass a lock. Repeat the process at the next bridge (No. 3).

The canal curves past the glasshouses at New Sutch Nurseries. Pass Moss Lock and then go under the railway line through an archway. At the time of writing, stalactites could be seen on the roof of the arch, formed by water percolating through from beneath the railway.

Just beyond the next lock is a grassed leisure area alongside a lane. Cross the wooden footbridge over the lock to the path on the opposite bank. Walk up past the top locks to arrive at the main line of the canal. On the left is an old dry dock. A signpost on the far side of the canal shows several destinations and their mileages. Turn left and walk along the towing-path for some 200 yards to reach Glover's Bridge again. Cross the bridge.

Turn right at the road and return to Burscough Junction by walking uphill and turning right along Junction Lane. (Before walking over the narrow bridge to the station, it is safer to cross the road and make use of the pavement).

Cottages and old dock, Rufford Branch Junction, Burscough

Burscough

The town developed in two distinct areas. The old village of Burscough grew along the Liverpool-Preston road, widened and turnpiked in 1771. The village later came to be known as 'Burscough Town'. A second township, 'Burscough Bridge', later developed about a mile to the north, near the canal bridge.

The landscape of Burscough is influenced by the two railway routes passing through the town, each having its own station. The line between Ormskirk and Preston uses Burscough Junction station, opened in 1849. The Southport-Wigan line uses Burscough Bridge, opened in 1855.

Burscough is an important centre for agricultural produce, particularly for potatoes.

Ashurst Beacon

The beacon was built on Ashurst Hill during the Napoleonic wars. It was expected that French forces were likely to attempt an invasion. The beacon was used as a watch-tower, manned day and night. The sentries were under orders to light a fire on the hill should French soldiers be spotted below.

Hoscar

The name of the village comes from the earlier name of 'Horskar', meaning 'horse-swamp'. Hoscar Moss, together with much of the land near Rufford and Burscough, used to be a marshy morass. It was drained to provide an excellent rich peaty soil.

Work on the drainage of nearby Martin Mere and the surrounding marshlands was begun in 1692 by Thomas Fleetwood. Drainage channels were cut. Flood gates were built and made to close against the tides coming up the Ribble estuary into the Mere. In 1853 a steam engine was introduced to pump water out into the sea at Crossens. Over the years, further drainage work has proved to be necessary. The Douglas burst its banks in the years 1877, 1896, 1927, and as recently as 1954. Floods can still occur on a small scale, but engineering work has made them less likely.

The railway station at Hoscar was opened in 1870. Until 1900 it was called 'Hoscar Moss' station.

11. PARBOLD – GILLIBRAND – APPLEY BRIDGE – LEEDS & LIVERPOOL CANAL – PARBOLD

A canal and country ramble along the Douglas Valley.

Distance: 7¹/₂ miles

Allow: 3 hours

Start: Parbold Railway Station (O.S. Ref: SD 491108)

From the railway station at **Parbold**, walk along past the two bank buildings. Cross the road. The road bends to the left, past a row of shops set back from it. Take the first right turn, up Tan House Lane.

Walk uphill for about 400 yards to a T-junction. Turn right, past a school towards the church. Pass the convent of Notre Dame. Just beyond is the Church of Our Lady and All Saints.

Continue along the road to reach a road junction. Turn right and walk along Alder Lane. After a few yards, turn left into Wood Lane. Ashurst Hill and its beacon come into view on the right, across the Douglas valley. The canal and the River Douglas flow along the valley floor, beyond the Southport-Wigan railway.

Pass a row of houses with extensive gardens. when the lane narrows, continue forward in your original direction, along a tree-lined lane. Ignore the "Private Road" signs – the lane is a public footpath. The land up on the left is the site of the old **Parbold Quarries.**

The way becomes a stony track between fields. On the right, over the valley, stands the tall chimney of a factory in Dalton. On the left of the track are the remains of the quarries, now covered with trees.

The track passes through an area of woodland. The dry stone wall along the left side of the track was probably built from stone quarried on the hill above. Go forward past Gillibrand House. Continue forward and cross a stile.

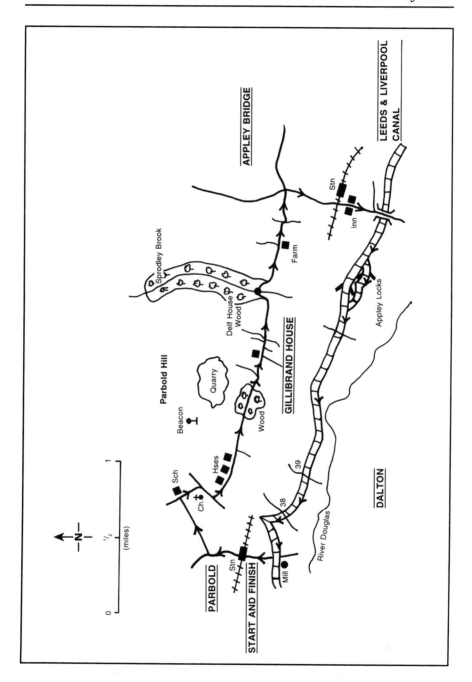

APPLEY BRIDGE

LEEDS & LIVERPOOL CANAL

Stn

Inn

Sprodley Brook

Farm

Delf House Wood

Parbold Hill

Quarry

GILLIBRAND HOUSE

Wood

Beacon

Appley Locks

Sch

Ch.

Hses

39

38

DALTON

River Douglas

N

½

(miles)

0

1

PARBOLD

Stn

START AND FINISH

Mill

Go along the narrow path through the trees. Cross a stream via a footbridge. Beyond the bridge, bear slightly left, alongside a fence and the edge of the wood. Cross a stile, and go directly across the road, rejoining the footpath on the opposite side.

Walk up alongside the fence, to reach a cross-fence at the top of the slope. Bear slightly to the right, and cross the stile into a field. As you walk along the edge of the wood, Appley Bridge comes into view. Continue along the right-hand boundaries of the hilly fields.

Reach the place where the fence and the line of trees end. Do **not** go down to the right. Instead, turn left and uphill for about 75 yards to an old stile at the end of a stone wall. This stile indicates your direction. Cross the field to reach a wood.

Go over the stile and down some steps. The path runs leftwards and through Delf House Wood. You reach a pavement and then a footbridge. Use the bridge to cross **Sprodley Brook**.

Beyond the bridge, climb the flight of stone steps. At the top, turn to the immediate right, and walk up alongside the fence to arrive at a narrow road. Turn right and approach the gateway of a farm. Look for a stile and steps, situated next to the left post of the farm's entrance gate.

Climb over the stile into the field. The footpath then runs alongside a hedgerow at the right boundary of the field. Follow the path, to pass behind Draper's Farm House, over a stile, on to a lane. Cross directly over the lane, and follow the path on the opposite side.

The path leads you over a stile, and then reaches a second tarmac lane. Here, turn right for about 30 yards only, before turning sharp left along a field-path. The path runs behind a row of houses to the main road junction, opposite **Skull House Lane, Appley Bridge**.

Turn right, and walk down the road into the valley, towards the Leeds & Liverpool Canal. The road leads downhill to cross the railway line and reaches the Railway Inn.

Beyond the inn, cross the canal bridge on to the towing path on the far bank. Turn right, and begin the return leg of the journey to Parbold. The distance along the canal path is about three miles.

About 300 yards along the pathway, you arrive at Appley Lock. A second lock is passed, a few hundred yards beyond the first. The canal here was split into two separate channels in order to allow two vessels travelling in opposite directions to pass each other.

The next bridge carries a track which runs beneath the railway line through an archway. Keep onwards beneath the bridge.

Along the next section of canal, look for the River Douglas, which flows along to the left of the canal. It can be viewed by means of a short path leading from the side of the next bridge.

The section of canal between Appley Bridge and Parbold is arguably the prettiest section between Wigan and Liverpool. The canal was cut along the natural river valley of the Douglas. The section between Parbold and Liverpool was designed to wind its way along a single level of land to avoid the construction of locks.

Approaching Parbold, the spires of its two churches come into view. Pass under bridge No. 39. Beyond the next bridge (No. 38) the canal forms a V-shaped inlet. The path then curves to the left to reach the road bridge alongside the tower of the old mill. Climb up to the bridge. Turn right, along Mill Lane. The railway station is about a two hundred yards' walk from the canal.

Parbold

The village lies to the north of the valley of the River Douglas. The Douglas flows from its source in the hills east of Blackrod to Wigan. The river then passes along a narrow valley between the Parbold and Ashurst hills, before flowing northwards beyond Rufford into the estuary of the Ribble.

There are two churches perched on the slopes of Parbold Hill, each with its distinctive steeple. The church of Our Lady and All Saints, built in 1884, is close to the convent of Notre Dame. A little to the east, along the slope of the hill, is Christ Church, built in 1875. The church of Our Lady replaced the 'Douglas Chapel', which was situated at the foot of the hill, about two hundred yards north of the bank of the Douglas. This ancient chapel was demolished in 1878.

Parbold Quarries

Parbold Hill consists of the rock knows as millstone grit. The quarries were abandoned in the last century but traces of the old workings and spoil heaps are still visible, covered by vegetation and woodland.

A small beacon stands on Parbold Hill. It is much smaller than its counterpart which stands on Ashurst Hill on the opposite side of the Douglas valley. Parbold Beacon, known locally as 'The Bottle', was built in 1832 to commemorate the passage of the Reform Bill. The 'Reform Column', as the monument was known, fell into disrepair and eventually toppled over. It was rebuilt and officially unveiled in 1958, the cost of £98 being covered by the contributions of some 150 organisations and individuals.

Sprodley Brook

The brook flows down to the Douglas through Sprodley Wood and then along a narrow ravine, known locally as 'The Fairy Glen'.

Skull House Lane, Appley Bridge

Skull House Lane takes its name from a house where there used to be kept a human skull. It was stored in a recess in the kitchen wall. Various tales and myths surrounded the origin and magical powers of the skull. It was said that it was that of a woman murdered in the house. Others believed that whenever it was moved, it mysteriously found its way back to its resting place in Skull House. The 'Skull of Appley' attracted many curious visitors in days gone by.

12. RUFFORD – OLD HALL – LEEDS & LIVERPOOL CANAL – SOLLOM – RIVER DOUGLAS – RUFFORD

The walk begins and ends at Rufford. The outward portion is along the Rufford Branch of the Leeds & Liverpool Canal. The final part of the journey follows the River Douglas.

Distance: $6^1/_2$ miles

Allow: 3 hours

Start: Rufford Railway Station (O.S. Ref: SD 467156)

From the railway station at **Rufford,** walk along the road in the direction of the **parish church.** The road passes over the Rufford Branch of the Leeds & Liverpool Canal. Pass beyond the church to the A59 Ormskirk-Preston road.

At the main road, turn right. Walk in the direction of **Rufford Old Hall.** This historic building stands about 400 yards away, close to the road. The entrance to the hall and its grounds are on the right-hand side.

The next part of the walk is along the canal tow-path. To reach the canal, turn right on leaving the hall and continue for 300 yards along the boundary wall of the grounds. Leave the main road at the first right turn.

The lane leads into open country. Cross the swing bridge to the towing path on the far bank. Walk along the path in the direction of Sollom. The distance to be covered alongside the canal is a little over two miles.

This section of the canal is less used than the section south of Rufford, but it is well maintained. It is a popular venue for anglers. The towing path can in summer months become rather overgrown along some sections. Do not be deterred by the jungle of grass and foliage. The path is wide and secure underfoot, and it improves further on towards Sollom.

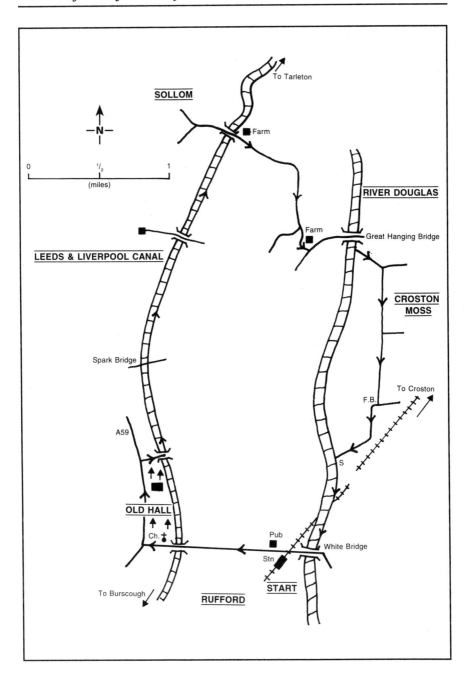

To Tarleton

SOLLOM

—N—

0   ¹/₂   1
(miles)

Farm

RIVER DOUGLAS

Farm

Great Hanging Bridge

LEEDS & LIVERPOOL CANAL

CROSTON MOSS

Spark Bridge

To Croston

F.B.

A59

S

OLD HALL

Ch.

Pub

White Bridge

Stn

To Burscough

START

RUFFORD

On the right side is the flat reclaimed land of Croston Moss. The Pennine Hills can be seen on the right. Winter Hill with its television transmitter mast is in view.

Pass beneath the A581 road at Spark Bridge. A swing bridge is reached, from which a path runs leftwards towards Fearn's Farm. Continue along the towing path.

As Sollom is approached, go under a line of electricity cables. The village is up on the hilly ground to the left of the canal. The path widens into a full-size cart track and you arrive at a bridge. At this bridge the canal joins the old course of the River Douglas. On the far side of the bridge the twists and turns in the waterway can be seen as it leads away to Tarleton, where it joins the tidal flow of the Ribble Estuary west of Preston.

Begin the return journey to Rufford from the bridge. Turn right and walk away from the canal along a narrow tarmac lane. After a short distance, the tarmac ends and the lane swings to the left. Here, leave the lane and walk forward along a cart track.

The track soon veers to the right. Running along the left side of the track is a narrow stream which flows along the course of the old river. It is a remnant of the Douglas left behind after the canal was built.

The bulk of the river's flow was channelled between specially-built floodbanks. This artificial channel now receives the water from hundreds of drainage ditches cut into the surrounding low-lying land.

At the point where the track begins to bend to the right, leave it. Walk along the edge of the field, alongside the old river bank. Follow the pathway as it swings to the right, along the edge of the field. At the corner of the field, pass between two large bushes into a second field.

Walk along the left boundary, and turn left at the first opening, at the side of the farm. An unfenced road is about fifty yards away. A large barn stands on its own on the far side of the road. Walk to this road.

Cross the road with care. Turn left and walk along the footpath for about 200 yards to reach the River Douglas at Great Hanging Bridge. Cross the bridge and turn right to enter a track leading leftwards away from the river bank.

This track later divides at a junction. Take the track which leads off to the right. This is your direction for about a mile across the level country. Looking back, on the right is the square tower of Croston church. A steeple of the church at Tarleton is occasionally visible to the left. As Rufford is approached, the hill on the left is above Parbold. Ahead stands Ashurst Hill and its beacon.

Eventually one reaches a T-junction of tracks. Go to the right, over a wide wooden footbridge, and then walk to the left, in the direction of the railway line.

Before the railway embankment is reached, the right of way goes to the right. Pass over a stile on to the left bank of the Douglas. The small buildings on the river bank are pumping stations. You can often see wild duck scuttling about on the surface of the river and birds fluttering skywards out of the reed beds at the water's edge.

Pass beneath the railway line via a concrete path. Reach the road at Rufford alongside White Bridge. Complete the walk by going to the right, across the bridge, to arrive at the railway station.

Rufford Parish Church

A chapel was built in 1736 on the site of the present building. This chapel became the parish church in 1793 when Rufford was separated from the nearby parish of Croston. The present-day parish church was built in 1869. On a wall inside the building is a memorial to William Hesketh which displays a verse composed by the English poet William Cowper, who was related by marriage to the Hesketh family.

Rufford Old Hall

The building was probably begun in the late 15th century by Robert Hesketh who was lord of the manor of Rufford from 1463 to 1490. The hall was extended in 1662 and in 1821. It was given to the National Trust by the Hesketh family in 1936. It is open to the public.

A building known as Rufford New Hall stands in its own grounds on the opposite side of the A59 road. Built in 1760 and enlarged in 1798, it is now used as a hospital.

13. WIGAN PIER – LEEDS & LIVERPOOL CANAL – ROSE BRIDGE – TOP LOCK – HAIGH LOWER PLANTATION – WHELLEY

A ramble around Wigan

Distance: 6 miles

Allow: 4 hours

Start: Wigan Pier (O.S. Ref: SD 582049)

From the Heritage Centre at Wigan Pier, cross the canal by using the wooden footbridge and go down the slope on to the towpath at the left side of the canal, under the metal bridge No. 51 (The Pottery Changeline Bridge).

You soon come to the Trencherfield Mill, its shrill klaxon sounding periodically. As you walk away from the pier, there can be seen a boatbuilder's yard on the opposite bank. As you pass Engine House Lock and the mill gardens, the cobbles give way to a smoother pathway. Continue past the metal traffic barrier and go forward to Chapel Lane Bridge.

At the bridge, climb the slope and cross the busy road with great care. Beyond the bridge the towpath passes a neatly-landscaped lock and some tiny canal-side cottages.

After about another 200 yards, reach a canal junction. This is the start of a seven-mile branch which connects with the Bridgewater Canal at Leigh, allowing boats to travel through to Manchester. The metal sign-posts on the corner display mileages.

Further along on the right is the modern Girobank building; it stands on the site of the old Westwood Power Station. After passing beneath two railways, the canal reaches the Warrington Road by the Shepherd's Arms. Further caution is needed when crossing this busy carriageway.

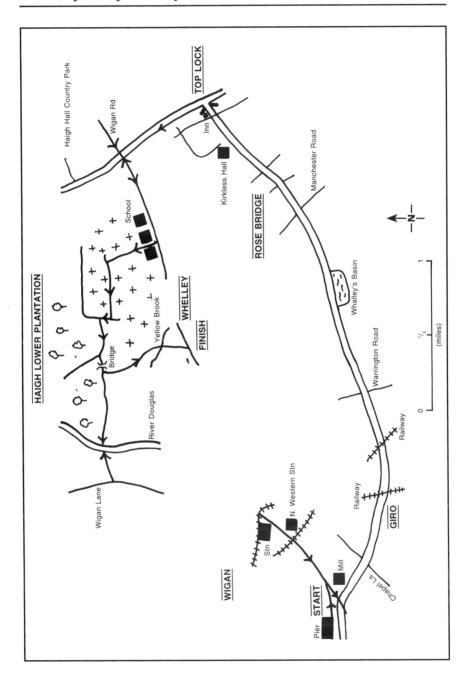

The areas of trees, shrubs and grassland along the canal banks have been planted in recent years to improve what was a previously blighted landscape, scarred by two centuries of industrial use. As you continue eastwards up the flight of locks, the woodland around Haigh Hall comes into view ahead.

Some of the locks have elaborate sluice channels to allow excess water to flow down past the lock chambers. Just beyond Lock No. 82, the large reed-fringed expanse of Whalley's Basin appears on the far bank. Numerous horse-drawn tramways, the precursors of the railways, used to run from local pits to the canal banks, where the coal was shipped on to barges. Tiny Rose Bridge Cottage stands opposite Lock No. 80.

After crossing the busy Manchester Road, the locks come in a tightly-packed sequence. The steep rise in level now becomes apparent. Another old cottage stands to the left, about 200 yards beyond Rose Bridge. The massive long spoil heap at Kirklees looms into view.

Notice that on the masonry of the lock chambers, an old numbering system is carved in Roman notation. The locks were originally numbered downwards, the Top Lock being the first of twenty-one locks leading down to Wigan Pier. Between some of the locks the canal was widened, allowing barges to avoid congestion at busy periods.

On the left by Lock No. 69 there stands a very old dwelling, part of which has black and white timberwork on its frontage. This building, which dates from the 1600s, is called Kirkless Hall.

On the next few bridges, their date of erection, 1816, is displayed on the keystone of each arch. As the woodland comes nearer, you pass the Commercial Inn at Cale Lane before arriving at the Kirklees Hall Inn.

A little way beyond the inn is Top Lock. The climb from the town ends here and the canal forms a T-junction with the incoming line of the old Lancaster Canal.

Continuing the journey to the left of Top Lock, the canal begins to head northwards towards Blackburn. To the left side and below you lies the sprawling town, with an unspoilt area of country leading out to Aspull Moor on the right bank. Ahead on the right is **Haigh Hall Country Park**.

Kirkless Hall

After some 400 yards, reach the bridge at Wigan Road. Look beyond the bridge and see an old building with an incongruously ornate cupola perched high above its plain roof. At the bridge, turn left and leave the canal at Withington Lane.

Do not cross the road at the foot of the humped bridge. Instead, walk down to the Crown Hotel and cross there. About 100 yards beyond the old school, opposite Cale Lane, at the town boundary, turn sharp right along a gravelled lane between the houses. Follow the lane as it curves away leftwards between paling fences. At a Y-junction, continue left-wards over the reclaimed site of **an open-cast coal mine**. (Traces of coal may still be visible in the top soil).

Follow the lane as it narrows down towards the woodland. At the fence, beyond which the ground falls steeply away, go to the immediate right, along the field edge. Then walk left, along a path to cross a wide stone bridge spanning a disused railway cutting.

Follow the broad tarmac carriage road. It leads you downhill through the shrub and woodland of **Haigh Lower Plantation**. The road runs down over the River Douglas to the main road at **Wigan Lane**. The walk may be completed there, or alternatively, turn left off the tarmac on the crown of the first hairpin bend.

The reddish pathway runs for some 300 yards, through a sheltered line of trees and then over **a fast-flowing stream**, past the houses at Plantation Gates to the main road at Whelley. About 150 yards to the left, across the main road, a bus back to town may be boarded at the Alexandra Hotel.

Waterbus at Wigan

Haigh Hall

In 1290 the manor of Haigh, which has been in the hands of the Norris family for the previous century or longer, passed to Sir William Bradshaigh when he married Mabel, the sole heiress of Hugh Norris. Sir William moved down from Bolton to live in the manor house and took possession of the surrounding estate. The Bradshaigh line of male succession ended in 1770 with the death of Sir Roger, the 4th baronet. The Haigh estate passed by marriage to James Lindsay, Earl of Crawford and Balcarres.

In the 1830s a new hall was begun by the Earl and was finished by 1850. Haigh Hall and the surrounding estate, extending to some 240 acres, was acquired by Wigan Corporation in 1947 and converted into a museum, art gallery and public park. In the recent past the hall and the adjoining land took on the role of a country park.

Mining at Whelley

The Bradshaighs were extracting coal from pits on their Haigh estate in the 1300s. The coal was a very fine grade of fuel called 'cannel'. Cannel or 'candle' coal was the best and most expensive household coal, found in valuable quantities in the Wigan area. Most ordinary Lancashire folk could not afford to buy cannel but there was a steady demand from wealthy homes. Large amounts were sent to London.

Cannel is a curious and remarkable material. Celia Fiennes, who came across it during her tour of Lancashire in 1698, described cannel like this:

". . . it burns as light as a candle – set the coales together with some fire and it shall give a snap and burn up light – of this coal they make saltcellars and standishes and many boxes and things which are sent about for curiositys and sold in London...its very finely polished and lookes much like jett or ebony wood".

A few years later, Daniel Defoe described his fascination for cannel in this way:

"Cannel coals will polish like alabaster; then a lady may take them up in a cambrick handkerchief and they will not soil it, though they are as black as jet".

The recently landscaped area at Whelley was first exploited in 1856, when the first shaft of the Lindsay Alexandra Pit was sunk. When the coal seams near the surface were exhausted, mining was discontinued. In the 1980s, coal was taken from beneath the abandoned old seams by opencast working, gouging massive black canyons out of the landscape.

The area is at the time of writing being successfully restored by infilling and tree planting.

Haigh Lower Plantations

The pleasure grounds were laid out in 1862 and 1863, at a time when the American Civil War had caused cotton imports to grind to a halt. Unemployed cotton workers were given the chance of earning some relief from their poverty by helping to create the plantation.

Wigan Lane

In 1651 a Civil War battle took place in Wigan Lane near Leyland Mill Lane. The land north of Coppull Lane was then countryside, with steep wooded slopes leading down to the River Douglas on the east side of Wigan Lane.

On the afternoon of August 25th, the Earl of Derby, accompanied by Sir Thomas Tyldesley, en route for Worcester, was riding from Preston towards the town at the head of a column of about 1,500 Royalist troops, many of whom were untrained Manxmen brought over from the mainland by the Earl.

Lying in wait on the banks of the Douglas was a Parliamentary force of some 1,300 men under the command of Robert Lilburne. These troops did not ambush the oncoming army but, as was then the custom, drew up in a mass across the lane. Determined to clear Lilburne's men out of his way, Lord Derby ordered his horsemen and foot-soldiers to charge. Unable to rout their opponents, the Royalists mounted three separate charges. After the third onslaught, Derby's men were themselves beaten back and tried to retreat up the lane. Lilburne had lined the hedgerows with musketeers whose withering firepower took a terrible toll of their outflanked opponents.

Wounded and unhorsed, Tyldesley was shot dead whilst trying to escape through a hedge. Lord Derby, with six other men, wounded in his arms and shoulders, fought his way through to Wigan and hid overnight at the Dog Inn in Market Place. Next morning, the Earl escaped from the town disguised as a trooper and made his way to Worcester. Half of his men had been killed and one-third taken prisoner.

Legend has it that Lord Derby's favourite beaver hat, worn over a steel cap, was picked up in Wigan Lane after the battle. Thirteen separate sword cuts were said to have been found in it.

In 1679 a monument to Tyldesley was erected at the side of Wigan Lane. Nearby Widdrington Road is named after Sir William Widdrington, another Royalist officer who perished in the battle.

The Stream at Whelley

The stream is called the Yellow Brook. It passes through a culvert from beneath the old Alexandra pit and then runs down into the Douglas. Before it reaches its destination, the stream is fed by water flowing through the Great Haigh Sough, a massive tunnel and rock cutting built by Sir Roger Bradshaigh in the 1660s to drain water from his cannel pits at Haigh. In the process, the clear waters of the brook are stained yellow by iron sulphide deposits washed down the sough from the old mineworkings.

14. BLACKBROOK – GARSWOOD PARK – CHADWICK GREEN – CARR MILL DAM – BLACKBROOK

This is a circular walk across countryside to the north-east of
St Helens.

Distance: 8 miles

Allow: $4^1/_2$ hours

Start: Blackbrook Road, St Helens (O.S. Ref: SJ 534966)

Begin the walk in Blackbrook Road, between St Helens and Haydock, at the canal bridge near the Ship Inn. Enter the Sankey Valley Park and set off down the path which runs alongside the Sankey Canal.

The path swings round a pond and then through a landscaped area towards Carr Mill Dam. The wooded hilly area over to the right is the site of an old iron-slitting mill. Excavation has been done to uncover its remains. The Blackbrook branch of the canal runs away to the left of the path, towards its terminus in front of the house.

The pathway takes you alongside the Black Brook. This stream spills over **Carr Mill Dam**, and flows down for a mile or so, into the Sankey Brook. The Black Brook was harnessed to provide part of the water supply for the canal.

Go forward under a road bridge. It carries the East Lancashire Road over the brook. Continue along the tree-lined path to pass beneath a railway bridge and reach Carr Mill Dam. Water cascades down steep conduits into the valley below.

Beyond the railway bridge, the pathway runs to the left for a short distance. Climb up the tarmac, and at the top, turn right and take the road which crosses the dam. From the road there is a good view of the dam and the lake.

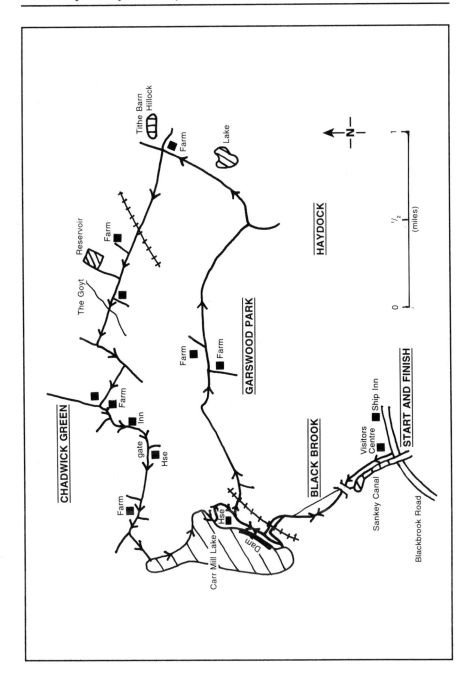

Continue forward along the track beyond the road, as far as the gates of the boat club house. Here, walk slightly to the right, and enter the footpath which runs behind the club house.

After about 200 yards, turn to the right, and pass beneath the railway again, on to a narrow lane in open country. After a short distance this lane joins the narrow Old Garswood Road. This peaceful byway winds for some two miles across the farmland of the Garswood Park estate.

About half a mile along, pass the entrances of Deer House Farm, and then Carter's Fold. Haydock lies to the right, a mile away across the valley. Follow the road as it swings to the right and climbs up to a T-junction.

At the junction, turn left, and walk along the pavement. After about 100 yards, look across to the right of the road, where a circular embankment surrounds a lake, on the site of old coal mine shafts.

Continue forward to reach the crossroads by Tithe Barn Hillock, visible beyond the crossroads. At the crossroads, turn left into Arch Lane. This lane will lead you across country to Chadwick Green.

Cross the bridge over the St Helens-Wigan railway. About 100 yards further on, pass the entrance of Arch Lane Farm. The grassy banks of Montrey Reservoir come into view on the right, at the side of a plantation of trees.

Arch Lane narrows to reach a junction which has some buildings to its left. Here, continue ahead on to a narrow signposted track. Follow the track between the fields. (In the second field, the public pathway runs along the left side of the hedgerow). The path dips down to cross a stream called 'The Goyt'. Follow the broad track to a junction. Take the left turn.

A sandy track winds downhill. Ignore the public footpath signpost and follow the road as it goes leftwards through **Chadwick Green** village, to the Masons Arms Inn.

Beyond the inn, the road soon narrows into a lane and you arrive at a gateway next to a cottage. Enter the signposted track through the gateway. This is your way back to Carr Mill Dam.

The path leads down to a second gateway alongside Otter's Swift Farm. The lake comes into view on the left. Go forward beyond the gateway, ignoring the track on the left. Look for a narrow path, leading off to the left, some 75 yards along. Its entrance is marked by wooden posts.

This path leads you along the shore of Carr Mill Lake. After about 200 yards, reach an **old aqueduct** which crosses the water. By following the path around the left side of the lake, meander back past the club house to the dam, before retracing one's steps through the park to Blackbrook Road.

Carr Mill Dam

The dam was built in 1826 to increase the supply of water to the Sankey Canal. It was built on the site of an old mill weir. In 1957, the remains of an old building were discovered beneath the surface of the lake. It is possible that this was the old mill itself. The dam was enlarged to its present size in 1860.

Boating began to take place on the lake in the 1920s, at which time a restaurant and a zoo were built on the lakeside.

Chadwick Green

In the first half of the last century, like many villages around Billinge, Chadwick Green was noted for the manufacture of nails. The work was carried out as a cottage industry in which whole families were involved. Slit iron was bought from local foundries. This was cut and hammered into shape over a raised hearth in each cottage. The industry came to an end only as late as 1860, when machines for the bulk manufacture of nails had been invented.

Rivington Aqueduct

The aqueduct carries water into Merseyside from the reservoirs at Rivington. It is known locally as the 'nineteen arches'.

15. BLACKBROOK – HAVANNAH FLASHES – PENKFORD BRIDGES – EARLESTOWN

On this walk you can witness a landscape, which was for a time industrial, being converted back to its rural origins.

Distance: $5^1/_2$ miles

Allow: 2 hours

Start: Blackbrook Road, St Helens (O.S. Ref: SJ 534966)

Begin at the old canal bridge in Blackbrook Road, situated on the north-east side of St Helens, on the road to Haydock. The Sankey Valley Park visitors' centre stands a few yards from the bridge, between Blackbrook House convent and the Ship Inn.

Set off from the side of the road which is opposite the visitors' centre. Enter the footpath which runs from the bridge on the left of the Sankey Canal. The course of the canal curves to reach a footbridge spanning the canal.

Do not cross this bridge, but instead continue forward to a second bridge which crosses the canal over the remains of the Old Double Lock.

Cross the bridge and continue along the right bank of the canal. About 300 yards further, arrive at Callen's Farm, which stands above the left bank.

The remains of Callen's Swing Bridge can be seen on each bank. Some of its masonry has been put to use to make stepping-stones over the shallows. Keep to the main footpath, soon coming to Broad Oak Basin, on the right of the path. Coal from nearby Broad Oak colliery used to be loaded from the wharves of this basin, for export to Liverpool and to the salt works in Cheshire.

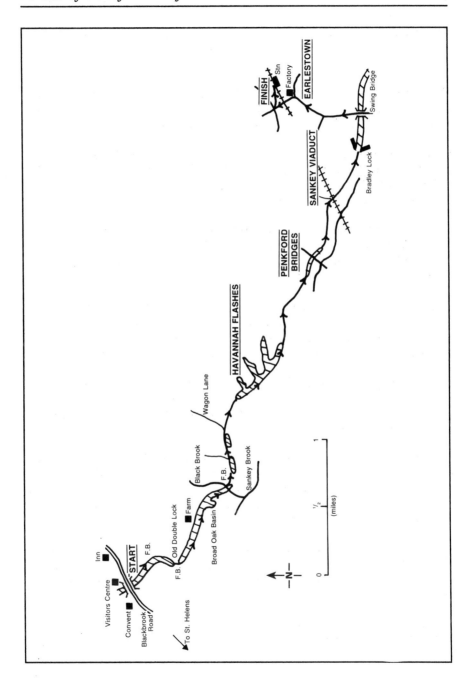

About 100 yards past the basin, you come to another footbridge. Several yards in front of the bridge, Black Brook runs into the canal on the far side.

The canal runs beneath the footbridge into the Sankey Brook, which flows away on the right. The channel was a side-weir to take floodwater from the canal. Now the whole flow of the canal goes that way.

Cross the footbridge and continue along the left side of the old course of the canal. (The fully-watered section of canal reappears further down the valley at Bradley Lock.) Several ponds remain to indicate the canal's original direction.

Pass the site of Engine Lock. Continue forward past a side-path which leads off to the left. A little further on, Wagon Lane leads away from your path. The lane gets its name from a railroad which used to run from the Haydock collieries.

Keeping to the main wide path, arrive at several large expanses of water. These are known as the Havannah Flashes. They were formed from water flooding into subsided mineworkings. This area is a popular spot for anglers. The wooded area on the far side leads towards Haydock.

Beyond the flashes, keep along the side of the old canal by entering a narrower section of footpath. For about a mile, the canal is almost completely dewatered. Reed beds abound, together with a wide variety of grass and shrubland.

Pass beyond a brick shelter at the side of the path. The country broadens out to reveal large areas of landscaped spoil heaps. Some of these have been reclaimed for agricultural use. Continue forward to pass through a metal gateway. Just beyond the gateway is another short watered section of canal.

One soon arrives at Penkford Bridges. Here the canal and brook used to flow under two separate road bridges. A tiny cottage stands on the canal bank at the bridge. These bridges mark the boundary between Merseyside and Cheshire.

Go forward across the road to continue the walk to Earlestown. A few yards beyond the bridge, the footpath passes over a series of brick arches. The arches used to provide a channel through which many excess canal water could be diverted into Sankey Brook.

Along the next section of the walk, you can see that the canal used to run for some distance along an embankment, raised above the level of the brook.

When you reach a tarmac lane which leads off to the right, do **not** enter it, but instead continue ahead along the footpath. The massive Sankey Viaduct is now in view. The viaduct was built to the design of Robert Stephenson in 1829, to carry the first Liverpool-Manchester railway over the valley.

Sankey Railway Viaduct

Approaching the viaduct slowly on foot, its lines and symmetry can be fully appreciated. The brook flows under the third arch from the right. The canal used to pass under the third from the left, where the footpath now travels.

Some 400 yards beyond the viaduct, you arrive at a wooden barrier. Pass through the opening and keep to the footpath as it curves to the left. The site of the old Sankey sugar refinery is upon the high ground to the left. Continue along the wooded grassland to reach the fully-watered canal again at Bradley Lock. One of the lock gates is still in position.

A short distance past the lock, cross the canal over Bradley Swing Bridge. Walk up along the pathway out of the valley towards Earlestown. Follow the tarmac path. It curves to the left to reach Junction Lane. Turn right and walk up over the railway bridge.

At the main road, turn right again and walk about 200 yards to **Earlestown** railway station. Trains to Liverpool stop here.

13a. Earlestown

See Note after Walk 16.

16. SANKEY – BEWSEY – DALLAM – WINWICK – EARLESTOWN

The walk follows the course of the Sankey Canal through the Sankey Valley Park.

Distance: 7^1/$_2$ miles

Allow: 3 hours

Start: Sloop Inn, Sankey Bridges (O.S. Ref SJ 585877)

Start opposite the Sloop Inn, in Old Liverpool Road, Sankey Bridges. The bridges carry the road over the Sankey Canal and the adjoining Sankey Brook. The brook flows into the Mersey a few hundred yards or so behind the inn. The canal travels in that direction too, before running parallel to the Mersey as far as Widnes. The described walk goes up the Sankey Valley, away from the Mersey, in the direction of St Helens, to Earlestown.

At the Sloop Inn, cross over to the opposite side of Old Liverpool Road. Walk a few yards to the left, and enter a footpath which runs along the right bank of the Sankey Canal.

After about a quarter of a mile pass under a footbridge. The canal then curves to the left before reaching the A57 Warrington-Liverpool road. Cross the dual carriageway and continue along the canal path. For the next half mile or so, an extensive area of parkland lies on the opposite bank.

Walk up to the right and use the path which runs between the canal and the Sankey Brook. Pass a footbridge and continue forward to reach a railway viaduct. This carries the Widnes-Warrington line over the canal and brook. At the foot of the viaduct, the path goes a few yards to the left over a footbridge to reach the towing path again.

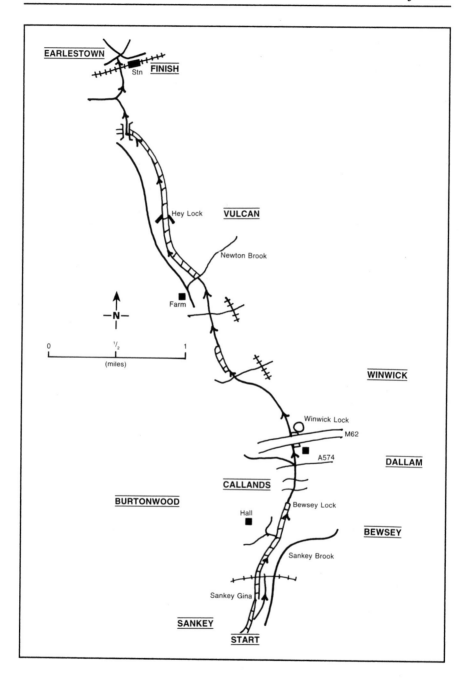

EARLESTOWN

Stn FINISH

Hey Lock   VULCAN

Newton Brook

—N—

0   ½   1
        (miles)

Farm

WINWICK

Winwick Lock
                                    M62
                                    A574   DALLAM

CALLANDS

BURTONWOOD

Hall   Bewsey Lock

                                    BEWSEY

Sankey Brook

Sankey Gina

SANKEY

START

The houses on the right are in Bewsey. Further parkland is passed by on each side of the canal. There are numerous reed-beds and pools, areas of grassland, lawns, shrubs and trees.

After about a further quarter of a mile, a lane and footpath are carried over the canal. Go over the stile and cross the bridge to look at **Bewsey Old Hall**. The old lodge is near the bridge. The grounds of the hall have been converted into a public park, and a new housing development is nearby.

Return over the footbridge to resume the walk along the towing path. After about 100 yards, arrive a gateway at the site of Bewsey Lock. A canal basin lies to the left of the lock chamber. Go through the gateway on to the bridge. This bridge used to swing on an axis to allow the passage of boats. It is now fixed in position. A good view of the walls of the lock can be obtained from the bridge.

Beyond the lock, the canal bed becomes dry. (A watered section of canal reappears later in the walk, beyond Winwick.) The brook swings away to the west and rejoins the path about half a mile further north.

Continue along the path towards Dallam. For the next half mile the path runs alongside the marshy canal bed. It then curves to the left to pass houses in Dallam. The canal's course then disappears, and you reach the left bank of the brook.

Continue forward along the side of the brook. To the left is the Callands area of the Sankey Valley Park. After some 200 yards, pass a footbridge and then reach a second one. Cross this second footbridge to continue forward along the right side of the brook.

About fifty yards ahead is a bridge carrying the A574 road. Pass beneath the roadway on the right side of the brook. Beyond the next footbridge, the path swings away from the brook. Pass through a further section of landscaped parkland and the path then runs parallel to the railway line.

Over to the right, the course of the canal reappears near an old sluice gate. This is the site of Hulme Lock. Do **not** turn right towards the railway footbridge. Instead, bear left along a grassy track towards the distant M62 motorway bridge.

The track runs alongside a fence towards the site of old Winwick Quay. In front of the bridge are converted warehouses with the date 1841 on the brickwork.

Pass these buildings by going forward along a wide track. Bear right, and then left, to go under the motorway. Beyond the bridge, bear slightly to the left and go forward down a pot-holed lane.

About fifty yards along this lane is Winwick Lock, a little to the right. If a gap in the fence allows, it may be possible to inspect the old lock. The timbers of the lock gates are still in position.

The lane continues for about a quarter of a mile to reach a tarmac road junction, alongside Causey Bridge. Bear slightly to the right for some 20 yards only. Do not go up to the bridge, but turn to the immediate left, and follow the field path which runs forward along the right side of a fence.

As this path is walked, you pass a short section of the canal's old course, before all traces of the canal disappear into fields. The path follows the direction in which the canal used to run.

After a further half mile or so, pass under a roadway. Beyond the bridge, do **not** turn down towards the railway, but continue forward along the path which runs about 50 yards from the railway. The path goes along the left side of the canal's old course.

Pass an old side-pond of the canal. On the left is Red House Farm. The land to the left of the canal and brook is in Burtonwood. **Vulcan** village lies ahead to the right.

One soon reaches a weir. Newton Brook is carried over the weir into the Sankey Brook. Cross the weir via the footbridge. A watered section of canal is then reached. The canal remains in water as far as Earlestown.

A few hundred yards beyond the weir are the remains of Hey Lock. Continue forward to reach a swing bridge. Cross the bridge and walk up towards **Earlestown**. Follow the path upwards and away from the canal. This path leads leftwards to the bottom of Junction Lane, by a small factory.

Turn right and walk up this road, towards the town. Cross the railway bridge, and then turn right. Walk along and take the second turning on the right, to reach the railway station.

Bewsey Old Hall

The first hall at Bewsey was built in 1264 by William le Boteler, the lord of the manor of Warrington. By the 1500s the building had been enlarged and equipped with a moat and a drawbridge. A new wing was added in the 19th century, but this was later taken down, so that the building which now remains is the Elizabethan portion.

Vulcan Village

The village is named after the Vulcan Foundry. This concern opened in 1832 as a works for locomotives on the newly-built Liverpool-Manchester railway.

Earlestown

Earlestown is a part of Newton-le-Willows which grew around the Liverpool-Manchester railway. First known as 'Newton Junction', the town takes its name from Hardman Earle, a chief engineer of the London & North Western Railway Company.

A wagon works opened there in 1853. It closed in the early 1960s. Earlestown was an important railway junction, situated at the meeting point of the first Liverpool-Manchester railway and the line from Newton to Warrington and the south.

17. SANKEY BRIDGES – FIDLER'S FERRY – WIDNES WEST BANK

A walk along the Widnes section of the Sankey Canal

Distance: 5^1/$_2$ miles

Allow: 2^1/$_2$ hours

Start: Sloop Inn, Sankey Bridges (O.S. Ref: SJ 586877)

From the Sloop Inn at Sankey Bridges, walk about 100 yards along Old Liverpool Road, over the Sankey Brook bridge to the canal bridge. Notice a small building at the roadside on the far bank of the canal. It used to belong to the Mersey White Lead Company. At one time, it served as a toll house on the Liverpool-Prescot-Warrington turnpike road. Turn left, along a broad lane on the left bank of the canal.

Pass through the gate and go carefully over the level crossing. The line carries occasional goods trains from Widnes to Warrington.

The canal curves to the right and then begins its straight course to Widnes. Go forward across a weir. It allows excess canal water to spill over into the Sankey Brook below.

Passing a footbridge, you come to a chemical works on the far bank. The upper broad lane alongside the line of trees provides an alternative to the narrow towpath. The cooling towers and the chimney stack at Fidler's Ferry power station come into view on the forward horizon.

About 200 yards further, with the modern housing at Penketh on the opposite bank, pass through an opening by a wide gate and continue along the improved tow path.

Heading towards Fidler's Ferry, the Mersey lies to the left, as yet hidden behind the high banked area. About 400 yards of walking takes you over the Whittle Brook. Ahead, and slightly left, the suspension arch of the Widnes-Runcorn road bridge comes into view.

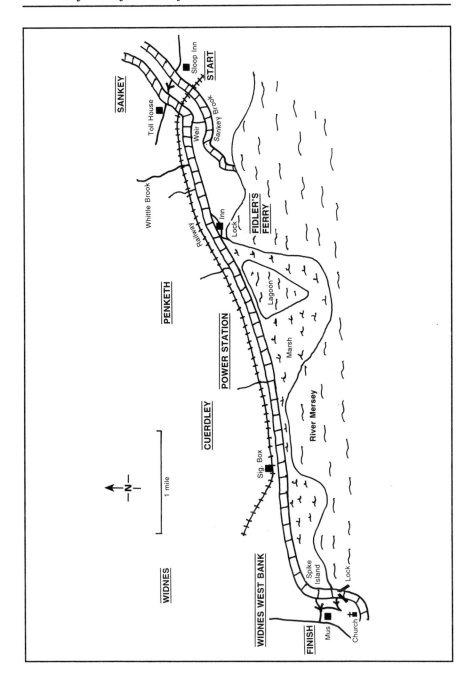

At the next canal bridge, notice that it used to swing into the far bank to allow boats to pass but, like all the bridge crossings on this stretch of the Sankey Canal, it is now fixed in position.

Over on the left a view over the Mersey will now have appeared. A hilly ridge runs out to Runcorn. High up on the far side, Halton Hill with its ancient castle stands up against the skyline. Other landmarks include the massive old water tower at Norton and, further left, the cluster of modern white buildings of the Daresbury research laboratories. Along the valley below the long ridge runs the Bridgewater Canal, between Runcorn and Preston Brook.

Continue ahead to reach the Fidler's Ferry Yacht Haven. The yachts are moored on the canal and sail on the river. Along the lane between canal and river is the Ferry Tavern. Tables outside the inn give a good view over the river. Beyond the inn is a large boatyard. A picnic area lies beside a slipway and an exit lock to the Mersey, through which yachts can pass at high water.

The Ferry Tavern

Resuming the walk towards **Widnes,** the canal becomes fringed with tall reeds and takes on a wilder appearance. About a mile further on, it narrows down to half width. To the left are the banks of the power station lagoons. Along a 300-yard stretch of waterway, the area can sometimes resemble a large garden, the canal forming a lake in front of a row of poplars making a boundary on the opposite bank.

The canal broadens out again and the towpath narrows. The Mersey and Halton Hill are partly screened off from view by a long hawthorn hedgerow. The Runcorn road bridge and the adjacent towers of the rail bridge are now clearly visible, spanning the Mersey at the Runcorn Gap.

As you pass the bridge by the old Carterhouse Junction signal box, the Widnes Marshes spread out towards the riverside. Cattle often graze on the foreshore. They wander to and fro through the swampy marsh with its hazardous network of narrow gutters.

Fiddler's Ferry yacht haven

The chemical processing tower on the right bank, with its intricate arrangement of steaming pipes and valves, is part of an I.C.I. factory which covers a large area of land next to the canal. As you go forward towards West Bank, the canal begins to curve to the left in front of the distant railway arches. At a broad wooden footbridge, you reach the extensive tract of parkland at Spike Island, through which gravelled walkways have been laid.

West Bank, Widnes, and St Mary's church

Leave the canal towpath and walk along the broad walkway. It passes along the river bank to an old square dock at the water's edge. Within the parkland, remnants of Hutchinson's soda works have been preserved, together with two of its brickwork arches.

Looking over the Mersey towards the Runcorn bank, a wide sweep can be seen. The small arch, low down to the left, belongs to a swing-bridge over the Manchester Ship Canal which runs along the edge of the far bank of the Mersey.

To leave Spike Island, cross the canal via a footbridge over the lock. Use the path leading out from the car park at the Catalyst Museum. Bear right, along Upper Mersey Road, past the Swan Inn and the medical centre, to reach the main Waterloo Road. Buses going towards Liverpool stop on its opposite side.

Widnes

In 1847, John Hutchinson, a 23-year old chemist employed at the Kurtz alkali works in St Helens, founded a soda factory at West Bank, between the Sankey Canal and the River Mersey. (A stone tablet commemorating the event has been placed on the site, now part of the Spike Island Park). Hutchinson's arrival marked the birth of the chemical industry in Widnes.

Hutchinson was followed in 1847 by John McLellan, a Liverpudlian of Scottish ancestry. He began to make borax using soda from Hutchinson's works. In 1850 William Gossage came from Worcestershire to open a copper smelter. After 1855, Gossage built up a prosperous soap-making empire based on his factory on the bank of the Sankey Canal, directly opposite Hutchinson's first factory. Around 1852, Frederic Muspratt, whose father James had a soda factory in Liverpool's Vauxhall Road, started making his own soda at the Wood End works on the north bank of the canal.

Chemical manufacture accelerated Widnes's growth. Originally a scattering of villages at Appleton, Farnworth, Cuerdley, Cronton and Ditton, the 1841 population of 2,000 grew to 3,000 in 1851. Ten years later it had more than doubled. By 1875, 20,000 people were living in the town.

The growth of the chemical industry from its beginnings along the Sankey Canal came because Widnes was ideally positioned. Coal came by canal and rail from St Helens. Salt came down the Weaver from Cheshire. Ores and minerals were imported at Liverpool and the finished products were exported from there. An abundant supply of water was available from the Mersey.

A large section of Widnes was built upon successive layers of compressed alkali waste. The town was literally built on chemicals. In the 1890s, government legislation was being prepared in an attempt to regulate the disposal of chemical waste and poisonous fumes. In Widnes's case, regulation was long overdue. In 1891 the Government Alkali Inspector came up from London to investigate. He estimated that about five hundred acres of the town's fields had been buried beneath waste tips to a depth of about twelve feet, comprising some ten million tons in all. The appearance of the Mersey at Widnes in 1891 is vividly described in the inspector's report. The river's waters were seen flowing *"between their greasy leprous-yellow foreshores . . . like turbid oil, with sinuous threads of scum on their surface"*.

Spike Island on West Bank, where the prosperity that built the town had its origins, is a popular place for local recreation. Many summer events are held there. The place is often enlivened by music and an ever-popular fun fair.

18. ELLESMERE PORT – SHROPSHIRE UNION CANAL – STANNEY – STOAK – CROUGHTON – CHORLTON – BACKFORD

The journey begins at the Waterways Museum in Ellesmere Port. It passes along the Shropshire Union Canal and through villages on the outskirts of Chester.

Distance: 8 miles

Allow: 5 hours

Start: Ellesmere Port Railway Station (O.S. Ref: SJ 403765)

The Waterways Museum is about a five minute walk from Ellesmere Port railway station. On leaving the station, walk over the crossroads past the Station Hotel. Continue down Station Road. The chimney of the pumping station at the canal basin is ahead. Cross the road. As you approach the flyover, walk along the old part of the road in front of the row of shops.

At the end of the old road, a subway to the right allows you to pass beneath the carriageways of the flyover. After emerging at the boundary fence of the canal complex, a walk to the right of about 50 yards leads you to the entrance of the Waterways Museum.

Should time and funds allow a visit to the museum, much can be seen in this area. A flight of locks runs down into the canal basin. Narrow boats are in evidence, some of which ply up and down the canal on pleasure cruises, particularly in the summer months.

Beyond the large grassed area is the Manchester Ship Canal. This canal begins at Eastham and runs along the edge of the Mersey estuary towards Runcorn, before following the old course of the Irwell to Manchester. Directly opposite, on the far side of the Ship Canal, is a

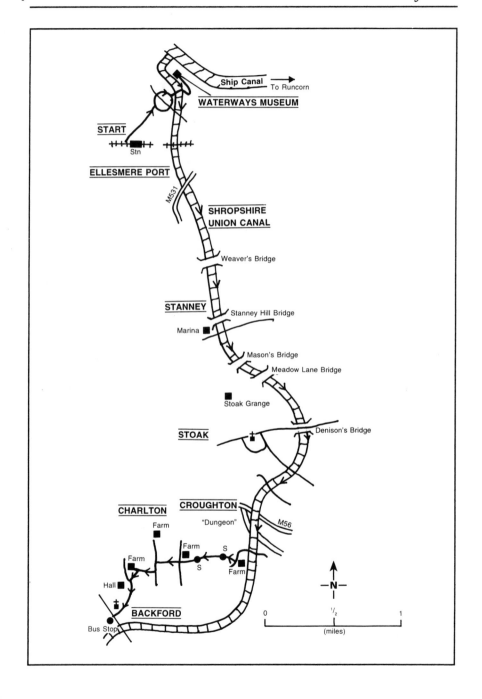

series of sluice gates which regulate the depth of water in the canal according to the state of the tide in the estuary.

Begin the walk from the towing path of the Shropshire Union Canal, opposite the museum entrance. Go to the left under a tiny road bridge. Some 50 yards further, pass beneath an old disused stone bridge known as Powell's Bridge.

The Canal Museum Quay, Ellesmere Port

The first mile from Ellesmere Port leads through an area which is entirely industrial, a bleak stretch of polluted water enclosed by concrete and metal, gasholders, motorways and chemical pipelines.

The landscape gradually opens out. Stanlow oil refinery is over to the left. The canal runs alongside the motorway to reach Weaver's Bridge. Beyond this bridge, to the right, are houses in Wolverham. The canal swings away from the motorway and after about half a mile Stanney Hill Bridge is reached. Just past the bridge is a boat yard and a small marina for pleasure craft.

The tower of the church at **Stoak** village comes into view ahead. The next two old bridges are known as Mason's and Meadow Lane. The large house and farm buildings of Stoak Grange stand to the right of the canal.

The view to the left includes the hills as Helsby and Frodsham, together with a rural Cheshire landscape leading away to the Peckforton Hills. The small group of houses about a mile to the left is in the village of Thornton-le-Moors. You arrive at Denison's Bridge opposite Stoak church.

The church can be reached by going up on to the bridge and walking up the lane. A path leads to the canal from the far right hand corner of the churchyard. However, on the author's last visit access to the towing path was hindered by barbed wire, so this way back is not recommended. Instead, retrace your steps down the lane back to Denison's Bridge.

Resume the walk in the direction of Croughton. The path passes beneath a series of bridges. About 100 yards beyond the second motorway bridge is an old hump-backed bridge opposite Croughton village.

Climb up on to the bridge, cross over the canal and walk along the tarmac road into the village. The road bends to the left. Look for a lane which runs off to the right, past the right side of a barn opposite the entrance of Top Farm. The barn was at the time of writing in use as a garage for buses. Walk up the lane and cross the stile into a field.

Follow the right hand boundary of the field, alongside a wooded valley known as 'The Dungeon'. The worn path passes through a gateway. Now go forward up the left boundary of the next long field. This field was being used as a clay pigeon shooting range with tall towers in the corners.

Cross the next stile, being careful of an awkward hollow just beyond it. Follow the left edge of the field to the corner. At the corner, go left and up through a gap to continue along the right edge of the next field. After passing through two gateways there is a crossroads in Chorlton, just to the left of Grove Farm.

Go straight over the crossroads along the Backford road. Walk along the right hand verge of this quiet road for about 400 yards to reach a sharp bend by the entrance road of Mount Farm.

Follow the road round to the left, past the bend. Look for a signposted path leading off to the right, about 100 yards beyond the bend. It is situated a few yards past a gate. Cross the stile into the field. Bear slightly to the right and follow the track which leads from the gateway. keep the hedge to your left.

Before the second field is completely crossed, go to the left through a gap in the hedge, towards a farm. Cross any single-strand cattle wire that may be fixed in the field and pass to the left of the farm buildings, past a large barn.

Beyond the buildings, go diagonally to the right, across several worn cattle tracks to reach a stile set in the hedgerow by the 30 m.p.h. speed restriction signposts.

Cross the stile on to the road opposite **Backford Hall**. Turn to the left and walk through the village. The road runs past **St Oswald's Church** to the A41 road. Buses for Birkenhead and Liverpool stop on the far side of the dual carriageway, alongside the small shelter. Reach your journey's end safely by crossing the busy road with every care and attention.

The Waterways Museum

The museum is built on the site of the once-derelict Shropshire Union Canal basin. The idea of the museum came from a group of canal enthusiasts who in 1970 formed a charitable trust called the North Western Museum of Inland Navigation. The trust set about clearing the long-neglected site. With the help of volunteer labour, the museum was able to open to the public in 1976.

A new organisation called the Boat Museum Trust was set up in 1980. During recent years money grants from the government, local authorities, and from the European Economic Community have enabled most of the old dock estate to be restored.

As well as housing a large collection of canal craft, the museum carries out restoration of boats using traditional methods. It has a large collection of documents relating to inland waterways. The museum runs an education programme in liaison with local schools. A conference centre is available for hire.

Ellesmere Port

The town began with the opening of the Ellesmere Canal. The canal was promoted by the owners of factories in North Wales. Their idea was to build a waterway which could carry coal, iron, and limestone to the Mersey. 1795 saw the opening of the Wirral Line of the Ellesmere Canal. Running between Chester and Ellesmere Port, it linked the Dee with the Mersey.

Pump House and Canal Basin, Ellesmere Port

For many years the canal area near the Mersey shore was known as 'Whitby Locks'. At first only a few dwellings existed. The growth of the town was slow. It was not until the formation of the Shropshire Union Canal Company in 1844 that the name Ellesmere Port came into general use.

The town's prosperity and growth was given a boost by the construction of the Manchester Ship Canal. This waterway opened in 1894. A host of industries were attracted to the town, which now had the advantages of good transport links with the interior, together with access to overseas markets, and an abundant supply of water for industrial use.

Oil refining expanded in the 1920s and 1930s. In 1955 the town was incorporated as a borough. Paper mills and a car factory were established. Between 1951 and 1971 the town's population more than doubled to a figure of over sixty thousand. Since then the town has retained its status as a significant port and industrial centre.

Stoak

The village has always been somewhat isolated in a corner of South Wirral. Stoak was described by Ormerod in 1816 as '. . . *a collection of filthy hovels, scattered round the church . . . on a small elevation adjacent to the marshes through which the Gowy forces its way to . . . The Mersey'.*

Drainage of the marshes improved matters and more land could be put under the plough. However, Stoak has as yet escaped much of the attention of developers and has kept its rural character.

A church is known to have existed at Stoak in the 1300s. The building underwent extensive restoration work in 1827, in which year a new tower was added. In 1940 an enemy bomb landed in the field behind the church. The windows were blown out, but the building otherwise escaped unscathed.

Backford Hall

The old manorial hall at Backford was rebuilt around 1810 by Edward Glegg. The manor of Backford, as was the case with many Cheshire villages, came into the possession of the Massey family soon after the Norman invasion. They held the manor until the 15th century, when it passed out of the family by marriage. The hall is at present used as offices by Cheshire County Council.

St Oswald's Church, Backford

A church at Backford was given by the Masseys to the newly-established Birkenhead Priory during the reign of Henry II. The present church was largely rebuilt in 1728. There is a triangular stone set in the ground at the base of the tower, directly beneath the clock face. It is inscribed: *'This Church Builded A.D. 1728, Robt Denson Vicar'.*

19. CHESTER – SHROPSHIRE UNION CANAL – CHRISTLETON – ROWTON – WAVERTON MILL – CHRISTLETON – CHESTER

A walk along the Cheshire section of the Shropshire Union network

Distance: 6 miles (or 8)

Allow: 4 or 5 hours

Start: Chester Railway Station (O.S. Ref: SJ 413760)

From the railway station at Chester, cross the forecourt and walk forward up City Road. After about 200 yards, reach the canal bridge. Walk over the bridge and go down a flight of stone steps leading to the left and on to the canal towpath.

Walk past the Old Steam Mill and go forward along the path towards the tall water tower in the distance, walking beneath a footbridge which spans the canal. After about 400 yards, continue under the road bridge to reach Hoole Lane Lock.

You soon pass a row of canal-side cottages at the Boughton. Continuing beyond the water works, arrive at Chemistry Lock with its adjoining old lock-keeper's cottage, still in use as a dwelling. (Notice the side weir on the far side of the lock. Water runs in a torrent along the weir and directly under the cottage).

A further 200 yards or so beyond the lock, pass behind some late-Victorian terraced houses to reach the Bridge Inn.

At bridge No. 123 the canal goes under the A51 trunk road and you arrive at Tarvin Lock, its cottage standing on the far side of the lock chamber.

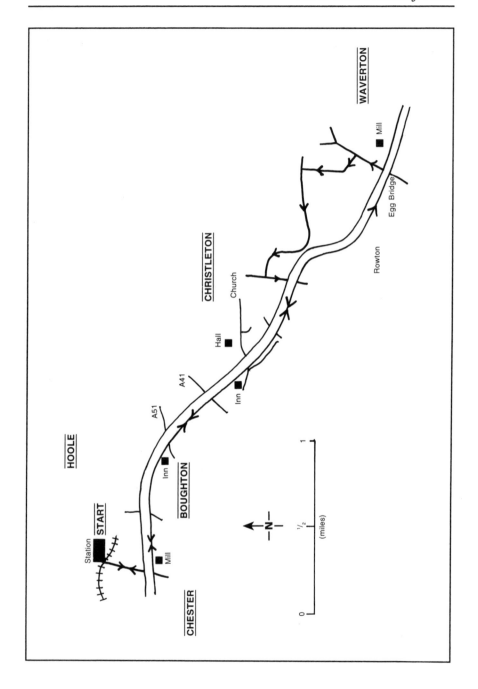

Shropshire Union Canal at City Road, looking east.

Beyond Tarvin Lock, so-called because of its closeness to the Chester-Tarvin road, the surroundings begin to take on a more rural character as the path leads you forward to Christleton.

After negotiating a rather uneven stony section of towpath behind the house gardens, walking beneath the next bridge brings you to Greenfield Lock. The pathway then widens and improves, past a second lock and under a flyover carrying the busy A41 trunk road.

A few yards further on, notice the first of a series of the original hump-backed bridges which carry numerous old lanes over the water-way. You soon arrive at the Old Trooper Inn at **Christleton**, a popular canal-side resort for boaters.

From the inn, continue ahead to pass the old mill, there is another narrow bridge. This bridge carries a lane which leads leftwards to Christleton Hall and the parish church.

Tarvin Lock

At the next little bridge, ignore the side gate and walk underneath. The canal then passes between open meadows. As the waterway gently curves, look over to the right to the distant sloping fields. Here, on the slightly rising ground, was fought, in 1645, the Civil War battle of **Rowton Heath**, watched anxiously through a telescope by King Charles I from his vantage point on Chester city walls.

The next bridge, No. 119, is called the Egg Bridge. Alongside it is **Waverton Mill Quay**, its refurbished old warehouses now converted into a cluster of modern dwellings.

Waverton Mill marks the eastward limit of our journey. The canal winds onwards through the Cheshire countryside, passing through Tattenhall, Beeston and Bunbury, towards Nantwich, connecting at Hurleston with a branch canal to Middlewich.

Begin the return journey by crossing Egg Bridge and then taking the first left turn between the houses, up Fox Lane. At the end of this short lane, enter a public footpath, over a stile. This path leads you over the meadows back to Christleton.

The first 50 yards of the path lead to a gate. Here, go to the left, following the field path over a series of stiles. After crossing the third stile, turn sharp left along the distinct pathway which brings you out on the canal-side.

Walk forward along the raised canal bank. Pass a double-pointed footpath sign near the water's edge, going over the stile. Upwards and to the right, look for a grassy mound with a stile at its left edge, at the back of the house. Walk over the sloping ground and cross this stile. It brings you out at Lane End Cottage in Christleton.

To regain the canal path, walk the 50 yards along the narrow lane and reach a T-junction. Here, go leftwards. Carefully cross the narrow humped bridge, watching out for vehicles which may be approaching beyond the steep rise in the roadway. Pass through the paling gate at the far side of the bridge, on to the towpath.

To complete your journey either retrace your steps as far as the Trooper Inn (where a bus can be boarded for Chester), or, should weather and energy allow, continue past the locks and the Steam Mill to City Road and the railway station.

Christleton

The village's name may mean 'Christ's little town'. The red and white stone church of St James, built in 1887, is the fourth to stand on the site; its tower dates from the 1400s.

In 1645, during the Civil War, Cromwell's parliamentary army used the Old Hall at Christleton as one of the garrisons for some of the troops surrounding and laying siege to Chester. The village was burned down in the conflict but the Old Hall and the church survived.

Christleton was a popular overnight stop for narrow boats on the Shropshire Union Canal. Towing horses were stabled at the Trooper Inn. The name of the inn shows the village's connection with the Civil War.

In spite of its closeness to Chester, Christleton has kept the character of a village with its green, its large pond and numerous black-and-white timbered houses.

The Battle of Rowton Heath

In September 1644, Sir William Brereton's Parliamentary troops, then besieging Beeston Castle, advanced on Chester and surrounded the city walls. Garrisons were then set up around Chester and it was put under what was destined to be a long siege. A year later, in September 1645, King Charles II left Hereford with his royal guards and, travelling via Chirk Castle, managed to enter the city on its Welsh side.

Meanwhile, Sir Marmaduke Langdale had crossed the Dee at Holt with a relieving force of about 2,500 royalist cavalry. (The animals got over the river using a bridge of boats). Langdale's troops camped for the night on Miller's Heath, five miles from the city. Next morning, September 24th, they assembled on Rowton Heath. Soon after 5pm, the Royalists clashed with an assembly of Parliamentary troops – some 3,000 horsemen and 500 foot-soldiers led by Major-General Poyntz.

Although the setting sun was shining in the faces of their enemies and powder smoke was blown that way by a stiff breeze, the Royalists, overwhelmed, broke ranks and fled. They were chased through the Boughton and to Hoole, losing 600 men dead and 900 prisoners. Next morning, the king, having seen his forces driven from the heath, left the city for Denbigh Castle. Chester eventually surrendered to the siege, some four months later, on February 3rd 1646.

Waverton

Most of this old village forms a part of the Grosvenor family's Eaton estate. Waverton is very old; it was listed in the 1086 Domesday Book as 'Wavretone'.

Corn from local farms used to be carried on the canal. The boats tied up at the quay and the corn was ground at the mill. The quay was a loading place for agricultural produce grown in the district, most of which went by rail after the 1840s. The original humped Egg Bridge was replaced in 1930 to cope with increased traffic.

20. RUNCORN – BRIDGEWATER CANAL – NORTON PRIORY – PRESTON BROOK

The walk is from Runcorn, along the Bridgewater Canal, to its junction with the Trent & Mersey Canal at Preston Brook. The latter part of the journey approaches Preston Brook from the Manchester direction.

Distance: 8^1/$_2$ miles

Allow: 3^1/$_2$ hours

Start: Waterloo Bridge, Runcorn (O.S. Ref: SJ 509829)

Begin the walk to Preston Brook at Waterloo Bridge, **Runcorn.** The canal used to pass into the Mersey via a flight of locks on the far side of the bridge.

A short distance along the towing path you pass an area on the opposite bank which used to be the Victoria Dockyard. Some traces of the brickwork of the wharves can still be seen.

The view to the left soon opens out to reveal the Mersey. Close to the shore is the Manchester Ship Canal. The power station on the far side of the river is at Fidler's Ferry. The land on the Runcorn bank leads out to Hempstones Point.

The canal banks have in recent years been planted with trees. In the summer months this greenery partially screens from view the modern housing developments on the opposite bank of the canal.

It eventually becomes necessary to cross over a bridge to reach the path, which continues on the other side. Pass beyond Castlefields towards the wooded slopes of Windmill Hill. A modern estate has been built on and below the hillside. Look out for a large lake situated close to the canal on the right hand side.

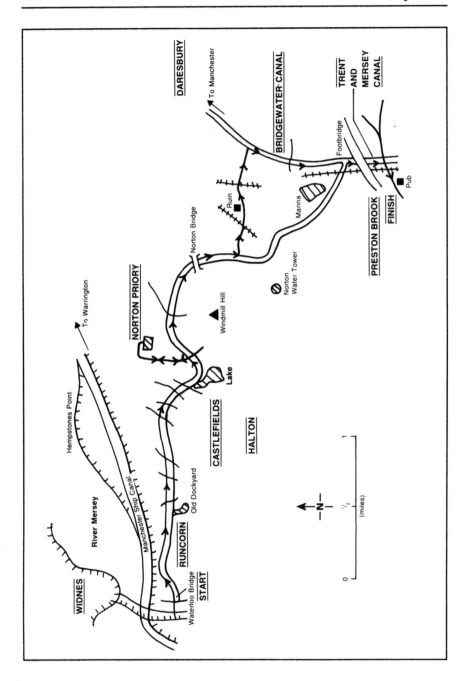

Waterloo Bridge, Runcorn

The next bridge beyond the lake is called Green's Bridge. It is approached along a section of canal which bends sharply to the left.

The remains of Norton Priory and its museum with ornate gardens are situated about 200 yards to the left of the canal. They can be reached by walking along the lane which leads away from Green's Bridge. The lane passes over a large grassed area opened as a public park. The priory grounds are on the right side of the lane.

The canal walk can be resumed from Green's Bridge. There is a plaque fixed to the arch of the bridge. It commemorates a rally held in 1977 by the Bridgewater Cruising Club in the year of the Queen's Silver Jubilee.

The next bridge passed is called North Townfield. The towing path narrows a good deal before reaching Norton Bridge. The original structure is no longer used, and has been replaced by a newer one. A change of sides is again necessary here, in order to continue along the towing path which resumes on the left bank. On the left is Keckwick Hill. The cluster of buildings with the tall tower are the research laboratories at **Daresbury.**

From the bridge which comes after Norton Bridge, the walk takes you to the left, away from the canal, across a short section of country, to the arm of the Bridgewater which approaches Preston Brook from the direction of Manchester.

The line of electricity pylons shows the direction of this section of the canal. The distance between the two sections of waterway is less than a mile. Go up to the bridge and enter the signposted footpath which leads off to the left. Pass under a railway arch and continue across the field. Pass a fenced-off parcel of land on which a farmhouse once stood.

Go forward over a footbridge. This bridge crosses Keckwick Brook. The path winds to the left and then to the right, and a second footbridge is crossed.

Pass under a second railway line. Cross the field beyond the railway, and climb up the steps to reach the Manchester-Preston Brook section of the Bridgewater Canal.

Turn right, and walk along the towing path towards Preston Brook. It appears that this section of canal is built on a much higher level than the other section. In fact, the water levels in both sections are identical. The Bridgewater Canal runs on a single level from Manchester to Runcorn without any locks. To achieve this, many high embankments had to be built.

Approaching Preston Brook, **Norton Water Tower** can be seen on the hilltop to the right. Below the slopes of this hillside are the modern houses in Murdishaw. A marina for pleasure craft lies to the right, on the opposite arm of the canal.

The junction between the Bridgewater Canal and the Trent & Mersey Canal is situated a few yards in front of the motorway bridge. Continue forward under the motorway to reach the centre of the village, with its modernised old cottages to the right.

It can be noticed that the Trent & Mersey Canal is much narrower than the Bridgewater. This difference in width meant that goods passing to and from the Midlands had often to be transhipped at Preston Brook between narrow boats and the larger Mersey flats. The canal divides the village into two parts. Preston-on-the-Hill, the older part, is on the high ground to the left of the narrow road bridge.

Buses back to Runcorn stop outside the Red Lion, situated a short distance away to the right of the road bridge.

Runcorn

Runcorn began as a small farming community. In the 18th century it developed into a canal port. When the canal trade dwindled, overseas trade developed and Runcorn became a centre for the manufacture of chemicals. Since the 1960s Runcorn has expanded further by the building of Runcorn New Town.

Runcorn road bridge

A town existed at Runcorn in 916. A fortress was built on a rock, on the edge of the Mersey at Runcorn Gap, near the present bridges. The fortress was built by a Mercian princess called Ethelfleda. She was involved in military struggles with the Viking settlers. Its purpose was to occupy and defend the narrow river crossing between Runcorn and the opposite bank of the Mersey. In 1115 the Baron of Halton built an Augustinian priory at Runcorn. In 1134 it was moved a few miles east to form Norton Priory.

In the 14th and 15th centuries ships set out from Runcorn to trade at Dublin, Beaumaris, and other North Wales ports. Until the coming of the Bridgewater Canal, Runcorn was a small agricultural village. Stone quarries operated on the hill.

The Bridgewater Canal transformed Runcorn into an important place for the transhipment of goods between the canal and the Mersey estuary. A staircase of ten locks was built to connect the Bridgewater with the Mersey. The locks were completed in 1773. The Bridgewater was opened from Runcorn to Manchester in 1776.

A system of docks grew up below the locks. The Bridgewater Canal built up a steady flow of goods to and from the Midlands via the Trent & Mersey Canal, which it joins at Preston Brook. Coal, stone and pottery came down to Runcorn. Cargoes such as cotton, wool, sugar, grain and timber went to the Midlands.

The canal port of Runcorn grew steadily. Further docks were built, and in 1828 a new flight of locks led down to a larger basin. In 1804, the Mersey & Irwell Navigation Company built a canal from Latchford, near Warrington, to a new dock system a mile or so from the Bridgewater Docks. In 1810 the latter were connected to the River Weaver at Weston Point by the construction of the short Runcorn-Weston Canal. In the 1830s and the 1840s, shipyards and chemical works began to operate in Runcorn.

In 1885 the Bridgewater Canal was bought by the newly-formed Manchester Ship Canal Company. As traffic on the Bridgewater diminished, the Ship Canal began to develop Runcorn into a port engaged in trade with Europe. The new port system provided the facilities for the export of salt and chemicals to continental ports.

By the 1960s commercial traffic on the Bridgewater had virtually ceased. In 1966 the Ship Canal Company filled in some of the old docks and blocked the connection from the Bridgewater to the docks.

Runcorn has become an important centre for industrial chemicals. The Runcorn-Widnes road bridge was completed in 1961. It replaced the old transporter bridge. The new bridge provided Runcorn with an improved system of road links via the motorways. In 1964 Runcorn was designated as an area for the building of a new town. The town was intended to house people migrating from Liverpool. Runcorn New Town is still in the process of development.

Norton Priory

In 1115 the Baron of Halton founded a priory at Runcorn. The priory was moved to Norton in 1134. It was a foundation of the Augustinian Order, enlarged into a flourishing monastic community before being closed in 1536 by the order of Henry VIII and sold in 1545 to Sir Richard Brooke. Brooke demolished part of the building and built a large house on the site. During the Civil War the priory was attached by a Royalist force who were beaten off by the Brooke family and their tenants. In 1730 the Tudor house was demolished and replaced by a larger building surrounded by landscaped grounds and gardens.

The Bridgewater Canal runs through part of the Norton Priory estate. The Bridgewater Canal Act of 1761 prevented the canal being taken closer than 360 yards from Norton Hall. In 1770 the Duke of Bridgewater petitioned the Commons to waive the restriction clause, but he was unsuccessful. The Duke proceeded to build the rest of the canal. Brooke had an unfinished canal at each end of his land for several years. The pressure of public opinion was such that in 1776 he allowed the canal to go through, and accepted £1,900 as compensation.

The Brooke family left Norton in 1928 and Norton Hall was demolished. In 1970 excavation work was begun on the medieval priory building by the Runcorn Development Corporation. It was built of red sandstone, probably quarried on nearby Windmill Hill. The building was opened to the public in 1975.

Daresbury

Daresbury Nuclear Research Laboratories were opened in 1967 by Harold Wilson. They are a centre for research into nuclear physics. Work is carried out there by scientists based at several universities, including Liverpool and Manchester.

The village of Daresbury is the birthplace of Lewis Carroll, the author of the 'Alice' books. Carroll was Charles Dodgson. His father was the Vicar of Daresbury from 1827 to 1843. Daresbury church has stained glass windows depicting Carroll, Alice, and several characters from the books.

Norton Water Tower

This local landmark was built as part of the scheme for the supply of water to Liverpool from Lake Vyrnwy. The tower is over 100 feet high with a capacity of over half a million gallons.

Index

A

Accrington 27
Acton Bridge 11, 73, 76-78
Aikin, John 38
Aintree 31
Altrincham 32
Alt, river 84
Anderton 10
  boat lift 14
  Cana Basin 13
Appley Bridge 105
Ashton, John 3
Ashurst
  Beacon 102
  Hill 98

B

Backford Hall 145, 147
Barbridge 41
Barton 17
Barton-upon-Irwell 31
Berry, Henry 3
Bewsey
  Lock 4
  Old Hall 131, 133
Birmingham & Liverpool Junction 41
'Black Bear Canal' 18
Black Brook 1
Blackbrook Branch 4
Blackburn 27
Blackburne, John 3
Boardman's Bridge 4
Bootle 28
Bradley Lock 4

Bradshaw, Robert 35
Bridgewater Canal, the 31, 155
Bridgewater Navigation Co. 36
Brindley, James 32
Brooke, Richard 33
Burnley 27
Burscough 98, 101
Burscough Bridge 27
Butchersfield 18
Butty Meadow 11

C

Cadishead 21
Calamanco 17
Caldy 67, 69
Carr Mill 120, 123
Carroll, Lewis 162
Castlefield 33
Chadwick Green 122, 123
Cheshire Lines Path 86, 88
Chester 38, 149
Chester Canal 38
Christleton 151, 153
Clayton, Sarah 3
coal mining & transport 3, 7
Cowper, William 111

D

Dallam Brook 1
Daresbury 158, 162
Dawpool 68, 71
Dee, river 53, 65
Defoe, Daniel 117
Double Lock, New 4

Double Lock, Old   4   *I*
Douglas Navigation   25   I.C.I.   10, 138
Douglas, river   103, 108   Ismay, Thomas Henry   71
Downholland   91 - 93
Dungeon Point   48, 51   *J*
Dutton Bottoms   11
Dutton Locks   75, 77   Jackson, John   11

E   *K*
                                          Kirklees   114
Earlestown   128, 132, 133   Kirkless Hall   115
Eccleston   7
Egerton, Algernon   36
Egerton, Francis   32   *L*
Ellesmere Canal   40   Latchford   21
Ellesmere Port   40, 141, 146   Leasowe   55
Etherow, river   15   lighthouse   58
                                          Leeds & Liverpool Canal 22, 79, 84, 89,
F   98, 108, 112
Fidler's Ferry   136   Linacre Brook   28
                                          Lingard, Thomas   20
G   Liverpool   28, 31, 38
Garston   8, 46, 49   Llangollen   43
Gilbert, John   32   London Midland & Scottish Rwy   9
Glegg, Edward   147   London & North Western Rwy   42
Goyt, river   15   Lydiate   89, 92
Grand Junction Railway   77   Lymm   32
Grappenhall   32
                                          M
H   Mackay, John   6
                                          Maghull   84, 87
Haigh Hall   114, 116   Manchester Ship Canal   20, 141
Hale   46, 52   Marbury, William   11
   Childe of   52   McLellan, John   139
   Hall   49   Melling   81, 83
   lighthouse   51   Meols   55, 57
Halsall   96   Mersey & Irwell Navigation   17, 59
Hartford   11   Mersey, river   15, 46, 53, 139
Haskayne Nature Reserve   96   Middleton, John: See *Hale, Childe of*
Haydock Lock   4   Middlewich   38
Hesketh, William   111   Mode Wheel   17
Heswall   68, 72   Morduant, C.L.   25
Hey Lock   4   Moreton   56, 58
Hilbre Island   53, 65, 68
Holmes Bridge   17   *N*
Hoscar   98, 102   Nantwich   41
Howley   17, 63   Newbridge   11
Howley Lock   59   Newton Common Lock   4
Hoylake   53, 56   Nightingale, John   19
Hulme Lock   4   Northwich   10, 11
Hunt's   11   Norton   158
Hurleston   43   Norton Priory   157, 161
Hustler, John   27

O

Oglet	48, 50
'Old Quay Canal'	18
Old Roan	31

P

Paddington Bank	61, 63
Parbold	103, 106, 107
Parr	7
Partington	17, 21
Pickering's Boat	11
Pickering's Lock	75, 77
Public Transport	44

R

Railways Act	9
Rainford Brook	1
Ravenhead	6
Rivington Aqueduct	123
Rowton Heath	152, 154
Rufford	108
Old Hall	111
parish church	111
Runcorn	33, 155, 159
Runcorn & Latchford canal	18, 62

S

Sale	32
salt (Cheshire)	10, 11, 38
Saltersford	11
Sandywarps	18
Sankey Bridges	129, 134
Sankey Brook	126
Sankey Canal, the	1, 123, 134
Sankey Lock	4
Shropshire Union Canal	38, 141, 149
Speke	
airport	50
Hall	48, 50
Spike Island	139, 140
Sprodley Brook	105, 107
Stanley, Sir Rowland	71
Steers, Thomas	17
St Helens	7, 120, 124
Canal & Railway Company	8
Railway Company	7
Stickings	17
Stoak	144, 147
Sutton	7

T

Tame, river	15
Tarbuck, John & Robert	6
Tarvin Lock	151
Throstle Nest	17
Thurstaston	67
Hall	68, 70, 72
Hill	67, 70
Tollemache	14
Trent & Mersey canal	13, 155

V

Vale Royal	11
Vulcan village	133

W

Wallerscote	10
Warrington	59
Waverton	154
Waverton Mill	152
Weaver, river	10, 75
Weston Point	14
Whelley	117, 119
Whitby Locks	146
Whitworth, Robert	27
Widnes	137, 139
Wigan	28, 112
Wigan Lane	118
Williams, Edward	13, 36
Windle	7
Windle Brook	1
Winnington	10, 11
Winsford	10
Winwick Lock	4
Wirral Line	40
Wirral Way, the	69
Woolston	64
Woolston New Cut	62